Modern Critical Views

Chinua Achebe
Henry Adams
Aeschylus
S. Y. Agnon
Edward Albee
Raphael Alberti
Louisa May Alcott
A. R. Ammons
Sherwood Anderson
Aristophanes
Matthew Arnold
Antonin Artaud
John Ashbery
Margaret Atwood
W. H. Auden
Jane Austen
Isaac Babel
Sir Francis Bacon
James Baldwin
Honoré de Balzac
John Barth
Donald Barthelme
Charles Baudelaire
Simone de Beauvoir
Samuel Beckett
Saul Bellow
Thomas Berger
John Berryman
The Bible
Elizabeth Bishop
William Blake
Giovanni Boccaccio
Heinrich Böll
Jorge Luis Borges
Elizabeth Bowen
Bertolt Brecht
The Brontës
Charles Brockden Brown
Sterling Brown
Robert Browning
Martin Buber
John Bunyan
Anthony Burgess
Kenneth Burke
Robert Burns
William Burroughs
George Gordon, Lord
  Byron
Pedro Calderón de la Barca
Italo Calvino
Albert Camus
Canadian Poetry: Modern
  and Contemporary
Canadian Poetry through
  E. J. Pratt
Thomas Carlyle
Alejo Carpentier
Lewis Carroll
Willa Cather
Louis-Ferdinand Céline
Miguel de Cervantes

Geoffrey Chaucer
John Cheever
Anton Chekhov
Kate Chopin
Chrétien de Troyes
Agatha Christie
Samuel Taylor Coleridge
Colette
William Congreve & the
  Restoration Dramatists
Joseph Conrad
Contemporary Poets
James Fenimore Cooper
Pierre Corneille
Julio Cortázar
Hart Crane
Stephen Crane
e. e. cummings
Dante
Robertson Davies
Daniel Defoe
Philip K. Dick
Charles Dickens
James Dickey
Emily Dickinson
Denis Diderot
Isak Dinesen
E. L. Doctorow
John Donne & the
  Seventeenth-Century
  Metaphysical Poets
John Dos Passos
Fyodor Dostoevsky
Frederick Douglass
Theodore Dreiser
John Dryden
W. E. B. Du Bois
Lawrence Durrell
George Eliot
T. S. Eliot
Elizabethan Dramatists
Ralph Ellison
Ralph Waldo Emerson
Euripides
William Faulkner
Henry Fielding
F. Scott Fitzgerald
Gustave Flaubert
E. M. Forster
John Fowles
Sigmund Freud
Robert Frost
Northrop Frye
Carlos Fuentes
William Gaddis
Federico García Lorca
Gabriel García Márquez
André Gide
W. S. Gilbert
Allen Ginsberg
J. W. von Goethe

Nikolai Gogol
William Golding
Oliver Goldsmith
Mary Gordon
Günther Grass
Robert Graves
Graham Greene
Thomas Hardy
Nathaniel Hawthorne
William Hazlitt
H. D.
Seamus Heaney
Lillian Hellman
Ernest Hemingway
Hermann Hesse
Geoffrey Hill
Friedrich Hölderlin
Homer
A. D. Hope
Gerard Manley Hopkins
Horace
A. E. Housman
William Dean Howells
Langston Hughes
Ted Hughes
Victor Hugo
Zora Neale Hurston
Aldous Huxley
Henrik Ibsen
Eugène Ionesco
Washington Irving
Henry James
Dr. Samuel Johnson and
  James Boswell
Ben Jonson
James Joyce
Carl Gustav Jung
Franz Kafka
Yasonari Kawabata
John Keats
Søren Kierkegaard
Rudyard Kipling
Melanie Klein
Heinrich von Kleist
Philip Larkin
D. H. Lawrence
John le Carré
Ursula K. Le Guin
Giacomo Leopardi
Doris Lessing
Sinclair Lewis
Jack London
Robert Lowell
Malcolm Lowry
Carson McCullers
Norman Mailer
Bernard Malamud
Stéphane Mallarmé
Sir Thomas Malory
André Malraux
Thomas Mann

Modern Critical Views

Katherine Mansfield
Christopher Marlowe
Andrew Marvell
Herman Melville
George Meredith
James Merrill
John Stuart Mill
Arthur Miller
Henry Miller
John Milton
Yukio Mishima
Molière
Michel de Montaigne
Eugenio Montale
Marianne Moore
Alberto Moravia
Toni Morrison
Alice Munro
Iris Murdoch
Robert Musil
Vladimir Nabokov
V. S. Naipaul
R. K. Narayan
Pablo Neruda
John Henry Newman
Friedrich Nietzsche
Frank Norris
Joyce Carol Oates
Sean O'Casey
Flannery O'Connor
Christopher Okigbo
Charles Olson
Eugene O'Neill
José Ortega y Gasset
Joe Orton
George Orwell
Ovid
Wilfred Owen
Amos Oz
Cynthia Ozick
Grace Paley
Blaise Pascal
Walter Pater
Octavio Paz
Walker Percy
Petrarch
Pindar
Harold Pinter
Luigi Pirandello
Sylvia Plath
Plato

Plautus
Edgar Allan Poe
Poets of Sensibility & the
    Sublime
Poets of the Nineties
Alexander Pope
Katherine Anne Porter
Ezra Pound
Anthony Powell
Pre-Raphaelite Poets
Marcel Proust
Manuel Puig
Alexander Pushkin
Thomas Pynchon
Francisco de Quevedo
François Rabelais
Jean Racine
Ishmael Reed
Adrienne Rich
Samuel Richardson
Mordecai Richler
Rainer Maria Rilke
Arthur Rimbaud
Edwin Arlington Robinson
Theodore Roethke
Philip Roth
Jean-Jacques Rousseau
John Ruskin
J. D. Salinger
Jean-Paul Sartre
Gershom Scholem
Sir Walter Scott
William Shakespeare
    Histories & Poems
    Comedies & Romances
    Tragedies
George Bernard Shaw
Mary Wollstonecraft
    Shelley
Percy Bysshe Shelley
Sam Shepard
Richard Brinsley Sheridan
Sir Philip Sidney
Isaac Bashevis Singer
Tobias Smollett
Alexander Solzhenitsyn
Sophocles
Wole Soyinka
Edmund Spenser
Gertrude Stein
John Steinbeck

Stendhal
Laurence Sterne
Wallace Stevens
Robert Louis Stevenson
Tom Stoppard
August Strindberg
Jonathan Swift
John Millington Synge
Alfred, Lord Tennyson
William Makepeace Thackeray
Dylan Thomas
Henry David Thoreau
James Thurber and S. J.
    Perelman
J. R. R. Tolkien
Leo Tolstoy
Jean Toomer
Lionel Trilling
Anthony Trollope
Ivan Turgenev
Mark Twain
Miguel de Unamuno
John Updike
Paul Valéry
Cesar Vallejo
Lope de Vega
Gore Vidal
Virgil
Voltaire
Kurt Vonnegut
Derek Walcott
Alice Walker
Robert Penn Warren
Evelyn Waugh
H. G. Wells
Eudora Welty
Nathanael West
Edith Wharton
Patrick White
Walt Whitman
Oscar Wilde
Tennessee Williams
William Carlos Williams
Thomas Wolfe
Virginia Woolf
William Wordsworth
Jay Wright
Richard Wright
William Butler Yeats
A. B. Yehoshua
Emile Zola

John Milton's
Paradise Lost

Edited and with an introduction by

Harold Bloom
Sterling Professor of the Humanities
Yale University

Chelsea House Publishers

NEW YORK ◊ PHILADELPHIA

© 1987 by Chelsea House Publishers, a division
of Main Line Book Co.

Introduction © 1986 by Harold Bloom

Printed and bound in the United States of America

10   9   8   7   6   5

∞ The paper used in this publication meets the minimum
requirements of the American National Standard for Permanence
of Paper for Printed Library Materials, Z39.48-1984.

Library of Congress Cataloging-in-Publication Data
John Milton's Paradise lost.
    (Modern critical interpretations)
    Bibliography: p.
    Includes index.
    1. Milton, John, 1608–1674.   Paradise lost.
1. Bloom, Harold.   II. Series.
PR3562.J63   1987   821′.4   86-29891
ISBN 0-87754-421-2

Contents

Editor's Note

This book brings together a representative selection of what I judge to be the most vital criticism of John Milton's *Paradise Lost* that has been published during the last decade, reprinted here in the chronological order of its original publication. I am grateful to John Rogers for his aid in editing this volume.

Essentially the essayists appearing here owe their starting point to a great theoretician, Angus Fletcher, who in his *Allegory* (1964) associated Milton's mode of allusion with the ancient trope of transumption, a metaleptic substitution of earliness for belatedness which is the particular signature of Milton's stance towards his poetic precursors.

My introduction, published in an earlier version in 1962, is an attempt to bring forward again the High Romantic reading of Milton, and was written much under Fletcher's influence as he composed his seminal *Allegory*. His account of Miltonic transumption is developed antithetically in my essay here from my *Map of Misreading,* and achieves something close to a definitive statement in the poet John Hollander's learned treatment of the scheme of echo in *Paradise Lost.*

Patricia Parker and John Guillory, in very different yet related ways, can be said to carry on a kind of transumptive literary criticism of *Paradise Lost* in the next generation. Parker, subtly arguing for a more temporal and less teleological reading of the epic, traces the shadings between Eve and evening and relates them both to Milton's modifications of tradition and to later developments in what then becomes Miltonic poetic tradition. Guillory, analyzing the simile-allusion of Ithuriel's spear as an instance of transumption, moves the question of Milton's triumphant allusiveness into the crucial arena of poetic authority.

William Kerrigan, brilliantly reminding us never to forget that Milton believed in the Mortalist heresy, in which body and soul die together and are resurrected together, traces this Miltonic monism in the imaginative materialism that centers on the metaphor of knowledge as food, poetry as digestion, spirit as energy. It is Kerrigan's distinction that he is the first critic to bring together, fruitfully, Freud and Freud's favorite poet, Milton. Maureen Quilligan looks at Milton's invocation to Urania in book 7 of *Paradise Lost* and considers the question of whether women would have been thought fit readers of the epic in seventeenth-century England, and, if so, with what limitations. In the final essay, written with Gordon Braden, Kerrigan shows us Milton transuming all that is most vital in Renaissance erotic poetry. Capturing the beautiful image of sexual fruition for his great epic, Milton "consumes a great tradition, and gives it back to us as representation and as understanding."

Introduction

By 1652, before his forty-fourth birthday and with his long-projected major poem unwritten, Milton was completely blind. In 1660, with arrangements for the Stuart Restoration well under way, the blind poet identified himself with the prophet Jeremiah, as if he would "tell the very soil itself what her perverse inhabitants are deaf to," vainly warning a divinely chosen people "now choosing them a captain back for Egypt, to bethink themselves a little, and consider whither they are rushing." These words are quoted from the second edition of *The Ready and Easy Way,* a work which marks the end of Milton's temporal prophecy and the beginning of his greater work, the impassioned meditations upon divine providence and human nature. In these meditations Milton abandons the field of his defeat, and leaves behind him also the songs of triumph he might have sung in praise of a reformed society and its imaginatively integrated citizens. He changes those notes to tragic, and praises, when he praises at all, what he calls the better fortitude of patience, the hitherto unsung theme of Heroic Martyrdom. Adam, Christ, and Samson manifest an internal mode of heroism that Satan can neither understand nor overcome, a heroism that the blind Puritan prophet himself is called upon to exemplify in the England of the Restoration.

Milton had planned a major poem since he was a young man, and he had associated his composition of the poem with the hope that it would be a celebration of a Puritan reformation of all England. He had prophesied of the coming time that "amidst the hymns and hallelujahs of the saints some one may perhaps be heard offering at high strains in new and lofty measures to sing and celebrate thy divine mercies and marvellous judgements in the land throughout all ages." This vision clearly concerns a national epic, very probably on a British rather than a biblical theme. That poem, had it been written, would have rivaled the great poem of Milton's master, Spenser, who in a profound sense was Milton's "Original," to cite Dryden's testimony. *Paradise Lost* is not the poem that Milton had prophesied in the exuberance of his youth, but we may guess it to be a greater work than the one we lost, for the unwritten poem would not have had the Satan who is at once the aesthetic glory and the moral puzzle of Milton's epic of loss and disillusion.

The form of *Paradise Lost* is based on Milton's modification of Virgil's attempt to rival Homer's *Iliad,* but the content of Milton's epic has a largely negative relation to the content of the *Iliad* or the *Aeneid.* Milton's "one greater Man," Christ, is a hero who necessarily surpasses all the sons of Adam, including Achilles and Aeneas, just as he surpasses Adam or archetypal Man himself. Milton delights to speak of himself as soaring above the sacred places of the classical muses and as seeking instead "thee *Sion* and the flow'ry brooks beneath," Siloam, by whose side the Hebrew prophets walked. For *Paradise Lost*, despite C. S. Lewis's persuasive assertions to the contrary, is specifically a Protestant and Puritan poem, created by a man who finally became a Protestant church of one, a sect unto himself. The poem's true muse is "that eternal Spirit who can enrich with all utterance and knowledge, and sends out his seraphim, with the hallowed fire of his altar, to touch and purify the lips of whom he pleases." This Spirit is one that prefers for its shrine, in preference to all Temples of organized faith, the upright and pure heart of the isolated Protestant poet who carries within himself the extreme Christian individualism of the Puritan Left Wing. Consequently, the poem's doctrine is not "the great central tradition" that Lewis finds it to be, but an imaginative variation on that tradition. Milton believed in the doctrines of the Fall, natural corruption, regeneration through grace, an aristocracy of the elect, and Christian Liberty, all of them fundamental to Calvinist belief, and yet Milton was no orthodox Calvinist, as Arthur Barker has demonstrated. The poet refused to make a sharp distinction between the natural and the spiritual in man, and broke from Calvin in his theory of regeneration. Milton's doctrine of predestination, as seen in *Paradise Lost*, is both general and conditional; the Spirit does not make particular and absolute choices. When regeneration comes, it heals not only man's spirit but his nature as well, for Milton could not abide in dualism. Barker makes the fine contrast between Milton and Calvin that in Calvin even good men are altogether dependent upon God's will, and not on their own restored faculties, but in Milton the will is made free again, and man is restored to his former liberty. The hope for man in *Paradise Lost* is that Adam's descendants will find their salvation in the fallen world, once they have accepted Christ's sacrifice and its human consequences, by taking a middle way between those who would deny the existence of sin altogether, in a wild freedom founded upon a misunderstanding of election, and those who would repress man's nature that spirit might be more free. The regenerated descendants of Adam are to witness that God's grace need not provide for the abolition of the natural man.

To know and remember this as Milton's ideal is to be properly prepared to encounter the dangerous greatness of Satan in the early books of *Paradise Lost*. The poem is a theodicy, and like Job seeks to justify the ways of Jehovah to man, but unlike the poet of Job Milton insisted that reason could comprehend God's justice, for Milton's God is perfectly reasonable while the perfection of man in Christ would raise human reason to a power different only in degree from its fallen status. The poet of Job has an aesthetic advantage over Milton, for most readers rightly prefer a Voice out of a Whirlwind, fiercely asking rhetorical questions, to Milton's sophistical Schoolmaster of Souls in book 3 of *Paradise Lost*. But Milton's God is out of balance because Satan is so magnificently flawed in presentation, and to account for the failure of God as a dramatic character the reader is compelled to enter upon the most famous and vexing of critical problems concerning *Paradise Lost*, the Satanic controversy itself. Is Satan in some sense heroic, or is he merely a fool?

The anti-Satanist school of critics has its great ancestor in Addison, who found Satan's sentiments to be "suitable to a created being of the most exalted and most depraved nature. . . . Amid those impieties which this enraged spirit utters . . . the author has taken care to introduce none that is not big with absurdity, and incapable of shocking a religious reader." Dr. Johnson followed Addison with more eloquence: "The malignity of Satan foams in haughtiness and obstinacy; but his expressions are commonly general, and no otherwise offensive than as they are wicked." The leading modern anti-Satanists are the late Charles Williams and C. S. Lewis, for whom Milton's Satan is to some extent an absurd egoist, not altogether unlike Meredith's Sir Willoughby Patterne. So Lewis states "it is a mistake to demand that Satan, any more than Sir Willoughby, should be able to rant and posture through the whole universe without, sooner or later, awaking the comic spirit." Satan is thus an apostle of Nonsense, and his progressive degeneration in the poem is only the inevitable working-out of his truly absurd choice when he first denied his status as another of God's creatures.

The Satanist school of critics finds its Romantic origins in two very great poets profoundly and complexly affected by Milton, Blake, and Shelley. This tradition of Romantic Satanism needs to be distinguished from the posturings of its Byronic-Napoleonic cousin, with which anti-Satanists have loved to confound it. The greatest of anti-Satanists (because the most attracted to Satan), Coleridge, was himself guilty of this confusion. But though he insisted upon reading into Milton's Satan the lineaments of Bonaparte, Coleridge's reading of the Satanic character has never been equaled by any modern anti-Satanist:

> But in its utmost abstraction and consequent state of repro-bation, the will becomes Satanic pride and rebellious self-idolatry in the relations of the spirit to itself, and remorseless despotism relatively to others; the more hopeless as the more obdurate by its subjugation of sensual impulses, by its superiority to toil and pain and pleasure; in short, by the fearful resolve to find in itself alone the one absolute motive of action, under which all other motives from within and from without must be either subordinated or crushed.

Against this reading of the Satanic predicament we can set the dialectical ironies of Blake in *The Marriage of Heaven and Hell* and the imaginative passion of Shelley in his preface to *Prometheus Unbound* and *A Defence of Poetry*. For Blake the Satan of books 1 and 2 supremely embodies human desire, the energy that alone can create. But desire restrained becomes passive, until it is only a shadow of desire. God and Christ in *Paradise Lost* embody reason and restraint, and their restriction of Satan causes him to forget his own passionate desires, and to accept a categorical morality that he can only seek to invert. But a poet is by necessity of the party of energy and desire; reason and restraint cannot furnish the stuff of creativity. So Milton, as a true poet, wrote at liberty when he portrayed Devils and Hell, and in fetters when he described Angels and God. For Hell is the active life springing from energy, and Heaven only the passive existence that obeys reason.

Blake was too subtle to portray Satan as being even the uncon-scious hero of the poem. Rather, he implied that the poem can have no hero because it too strongly features Milton's self-abnegation in assign-ing human creative power to its diabolical side. Shelley went further, and claimed Satan as a semi-Promethean or flawed hero, whose character engenders in the reader's mind a pernicious casuistry of humanist argument against theological injustice. Shelley more directly fathered the Satanist school by his forceful statement of its aesthetic case: "Nothing can exceed the energy and magnificence of Satan as expressed in *Paradise Lost*." Whatever else, Shelley concluded, might be said for the Christian basis of the poem, it was clear that Milton's Satan as a moral being was far superior to Milton's God.

Each reader of *Paradise Lost* must find for herself or himself the proper reading of Satan, whose appeal is clearly all but universal. Amid so much magnificence it is difficult to choose a single passage from *Paradise Lost* as surpassing all others, but I incline to the superlative speech of Satan on top of Mount Niphates (book 4, lines 32–113), which is the text upon which the anti-Satanist, Satanist, or some compromise attitude must finally rest:

> O thou that with surpassing Glory crown'd,
> Look'st from thy sole Dominion like the God
> Of this new World; at whose sight all the Stars
> Hide thir diminisht heads; to thee I call,
> But with no friendly voice, and add thy name
> O Sun, to tell thee how I hate thy beams
> That bring to my remembrance from what state
> I fell, how glorious once above thy Sphere;
> Till Pride and worse Ambition threw me down
> Warring in Heav'n against Heav'n's matchless King:
> Ah wherefore! he deserv'd no such return
> From me, whom he created what I was
> In that bright eminence, and with his good
> Upbraided none; nor was his service hard.
> What could be less than to afford him praise,
> The easiest recompense, and pay him thanks,
> How due! yet all his good prov'd ill in me,
> And wrought but malice; lifted up so high
> I sdein'd subjection, and thought one step higher
> Would set me highest, and in a moment quit
> The debt immense of endless gratitude,
> So burdensome, still paying, still to owe;
> Forgetful what from him I still receiv'd,
> And understood not that a grateful mind

By owing owes not, but still pays, at once
Indebted and discharg'd; what burden then?
O had his powerful Destiny ordain'd
Me some inferior Angel, I had stood
Then happy; no unbounded hope had rais'd
Ambition. Yet why not? some other Power
As great might have aspir'd, and me though mean
Drawn to his part; but other Powers as great
Fell not, but stand unshak'n, from within
Or from without, to all temptations arm'd.
Hadst thou the same free Will and Power to stand?
Thou hadst: whom hast thou then or what to accuse,
But Heav'n's free Love dealt equally to all?
Be then his Love accurst, since love or hate,
To me alike, it deals eternal woe.
Nay curs'd be thou; since against his thy will
Chose freely what it now so justly rues.
Me miserable! which way shall I fly
Infinite wrath, and infinite despair?
Which way I fly is Hell; myself am Hell;
And in the lowest deep a lower deep
Still threat'ning to devour me opens wide,
To which the Hell I suffer seems a Heav'n.
O then at last relent: is there no place
Left for Repentance, none for Pardon left?
None left but by submission; and that word
Disdain forbids me, and my dread of shame
Among the Spirits beneath, whom I seduc'd
With other promises and other vaunts
Than to submit, boasting I could subdue
Th' Omnipotent. Ay me, they little know
How dearly I abide that boast so vain,
Under what torments inwardly I groan:
While they adore me on the Throne of Hell,
With Diadem and Sceptre high advanc'd
The lower still I fall, only Supreme
In misery; such joy Ambition finds.
But say I could repent and could obtain
By Act of Grace my former state; how soon
Would highth recall high thoughts, how soon unsay

What feign'd submission swore: ease would recant
Vows made in pain, as violent and void.
For never can true reconcilement grow
Where wounds of deadly hate have pierc'd so deep:
Which would but lead me to a worse relapse,
And heavier fall: so should I purchase dear
Short intermission bought with double smart.
This knows my punisher; therefore as far
From granting hee, as I from begging peace:
All hope excluded thus, behold instead
Of us out-cast, exil'd, his new delight,
Mankind created, and for him this World.
So farewell Hope, and with Hope farewell Fear,
Farewell Remorse: all Good to me is lost;
Evil be thou my Good; by thee at least
Divided Empire with Heav'n's King I hold
By thee, and more than half perhaps will reign;
As Man ere long, and this new World shall know.

Here Satan makes his last choice, and ceases to be what he was in the early books of the poem. All that the anti-Satanists say about him is true *after* this point; all or almost all claimed for him by the Satanists is true *before* it. When this speech is concluded, Satan has become Blake's "shadow of desire," and he is on the downward path that will make him "as big with absurdity" as ever Addison and Lewis claimed him to be. Nothing that can be regenerated remains in Satan, and the rift between his self-ruined spirit and his radically corrupted nature widens until he is the hissing serpent of popular tradition, plucking greedily at the Dead Sea fruit of Hell in a fearful parody of Eve's Fall.

It is on Mount Niphates again that Satan, now a mere (but very subtle) tempter, stands when he shows Christ the kingdoms of this world in the brief epic *Paradise Regained*. "Brief epic" is the traditional description of this poem (published in 1671, four years after *Paradise Lost*), but the description has been usefully challenged by several modern critics. E. M. W. Tillyard has warned against judging the poem by any kind of epic standard and has suggested instead that it ought to be read as a kind of Morality play, while Arnold Stein has termed it an internal drama, set in the Son of God's mind. Louis L. Martz has argued, following Tillyard, that the poem is an attempt to convert Virgil's *Georgics* into a mode for religious poetry, and ought therefore to be read as both a didactic work and a formal meditation on the Gospel. *Paradise Regained* is so subdued a poem when compared to *Paradise Lost* that we find real difficulty in reading it as epic. Yet it does resemble Job, which Milton gave as the possible model for a brief epic, for like Job it is essentially a structure of gathering self-awareness, of the protagonist and hero recognizing himself in his relation to God. Milton's Son of Man is obedient where Milton's Adam was disobedient; Job was not quite either until God spoke to him and demonstrated the radical incompatibility involved in any mortal's questionings of divine purpose. Job, until his poem's climax, is an epic hero because he has an unresolved conflict within himself, between his own conviction of righteousness and his moral outrage at the calamities that have come upon him despite his righteousness. Job needs to overcome the temptations afforded him by this conflict, including those offered by his comforters (to deny his own righteousness) and by his finely laconic wife (to curse God and die). The temptations of Milton's Son of God (the poet's fondness for this name of Christ is another testimony to his Hebraic preference for the Father over the Son) are not easy for us to sympathize with in any very dramatic way, unlike the temptations of Job who is a man like ourselves. But again Milton is repeating the lifelong quest of his poetry; to see man as an integrated unity of distinct natures, body and soul harmonized. In Christ these natures are perfectly unified, and so the self-realization of Christ is an image of the possibility of human integration. Job learns not to tempt God's patience too far; Christ learns who he is, and in that moment of self-revelation Satan is smitten with amazement and falls as by the blow of a Hercules. Milton had seen himself in *Paradise Lost* as Abdiel, the faithful Angel who will not follow Satan in rebellion against God, defying thus the scorn of his fellows. Less consciously, something crucial in Milton had found its way into the Satan of the opening books, sounding a stoic defiance of adversity. In *Paradise Regained,* Milton, with genuine humility, is exploring the Jobean problem within himself. Has he, as a Son of God also, tried God's patience too far, and can he at length overcome the internal temptations that beset a proud spirit reduced to being a voice in the wilderness? The poet's conquest over himself is figured in the greater Son of God's triumphant endurance, and in the quiet close of *Paradise Regained,* where the Savior returns to his mother's house to lead again, for a while, the private life of contemplation and patience while waiting upon God's will, not the public life forever closed to Milton.

Published with *Paradise Regained* in 1671, the dramatic poem *Samson Agonistes* is more admired today than the brief epic it accompanied. The poem's title, like the *Prometheus Bound* of Aeschylus, refers to the episode in the hero's life upon which the work is centered. The reference (from the Greek for athletic contestants in public games) is to Samson's ordeal before the Philistines at their Feast of Dagon, where he is summoned for their sport to demonstrate his blind strength, and where his faith gives him light enough to destroy them. *Samson* is Milton's Christian modification of Athenian drama, as *Paradise Lost* had been of classical epic. Yet Milton's drama is his most personal poem, in its experimental metric and in its self-reference alike. Modern editors cautiously warn against overstressing the extent to which Samson represents Milton, yet the representation seems undeniable, and justly so, to the common reader. Milton's hatred of his enemies does not seem particularly Christian to many of his modern critics, but its ferocious zeal fits both the biblical story of Samson and the very bitter situation that the blind Puritan champion had to face in the first decade of the Restoration. The crucial text here is the great Chorus, lines 652–709, in which Milton confronts everything in the world of public events that had hurt him most:

> *Chorus.* Many are the sayings of the wise
> In ancient and in modern books enroll'd,
> Extolling Patience as the truest fortitude,
> And to the bearing well of all calamities,
> All chances incident to man's frail life
> Consolatories writ
> With studied argument, and much persuasion sought
> Lenient of grief and anxious thought,
> But with th'afflicted in his pangs thir sound
> Little prevails, or rather seems a tune,
> Harsh, and of dissonant mood from his complaint,
> Unless he feel within
> Some source of consolation from above;
> Secret refreshings, that repair his strength,
> And fainting spirits uphold.
>   God of our Fathers, what is man!
> That thou towards him with hand so various,
> Or might I say contrarious,
> Temper'st thy providence through his short course,
> Not evenly, as thou rul'st

Th' Angelic orders and inferior creatures mute,
Irrational and brute.
Nor do I name of men the common rout,
That wand'ring loose about
Grow up and perish, as the summer fly,
Heads without name no more remember'd,
But such as thou hast solemnly elected,
With gifts and graces eminently adorn'd
To some great work, thy glory,
And people's safety, which in part they effect:
Yet toward these, thus dignifi'd, thou oft,
Amidst thir height of noon,
Changest thy count'nance and thy hand, with no regard
Of highest favors past
From thee on them, or them to thee of service.
　　Nor only dost degrade them, or remit
To life obscur'd, which were a fair dismission,
But throw'st them lower than thou didst exalt them high,
Unseemly falls in human eye,
Too grievous for the trespass or omission,
Oft leav'st them to the hostile sword
Of Heathen and profane, thir carcases
To dogs and fowls a prey, or else captív'd:
Or to th'unjust tribunals, under change of times,
And condemnation of th'ingrateful multitude.
If these they scape, perhaps in poverty
With sickness and disease thou bow'st them down,
Painful diseases and deform'd,
In crude old age;
Though not disordinate, yet causeless suff'ring
The punishment of dissolute days: in fine,
Just or unjust, alike seem miserable,
For oft alike, both come to evil end.
　　So deal not with this once thy glorious Champion,
The Image of thy strength, and mighty minister.
What do I beg? how hast thou dealt already?
Behold him in this state calamitous, and turn
His labors, for thou canst, to peaceful end.

The theodicy of *Paradise Lost* seems abstract compared to the terrible emotion conveyed in this majestic hymn. The men solemnly elected

by God for the great work of renovation that is at once God's glory
and the people's safety are then evidently abandoned by God, and
indeed thrown by Him lower than He previously exalted them on
high. Milton had lived to see the bodies of his great leaders and
associates, including Cromwell, dug up and hanged on the gallows to
commemorate the twelfth anniversary of the execution of Charles I.
Sir Henry Vane, for whom Milton had a warm and especial admira-
tion, had been executed by order of "the unjust tribunals, under
change of times, / And condemnation of the ingrateful multitude."
Samson Agonistes gives us not only the sense of having experienced a
perfectly proportioned work of art, but also the memory of Milton's
most moving prayer to God, which follows his account of the tribula-
tions of his fellow Puritans:

> So deal not with this once thy glorious Champion,
> The Image of thy strength, and mighty minister.
> What do I beg? how hast thou dealt already?
> Behold him in this state calamitous, and turn
> His labours, for thou canst, to peaceful end.

Milton and Transumption

Harold Bloom

No poet compares to Milton in his intensity of self-consciousness as an artist and in his ability to overcome all negative consequences of such concern. Milton's highly deliberate and knowingly ambitious program necessarily involved him in direct competition with Homer, Virgil, Lucretius, Ovid, Dante, and Tasso, among other major precursors. More anxiously, it brought him very close to Spenser, whose actual influence on *Paradise Lost* is deeper, subtler and more extensive than scholarship so far has recognized. Most anxiously, the ultimate ambitions of *Paradise Lost* gave Milton the problem of expanding scripture without distorting the Word of God.

A reader, thinking of Milton's style, is very likely to recognize that style's most distinctive characteristics as being the density of its allusiveness. Perhaps only Gray compares to Milton in this regard, and Gray is only a footnote, though an important and valuable one, to the Miltonic splendor. Milton's allusiveness has a distinct design, which is to enhance both the quality and the extent of his inventiveness. His handling of allusion is his highly individual and original defense against poetic tradition, his revisionary stance in writing what is in effect a tertiary epic, following after Homer in primary epic and Virgil, Ovid, and Dante in secondary epic. Most vitally, Miltonic allusion is the crucial revisionary ratio by which *Paradise Lost* distances itself from its most dangerous precursor, *The Faerie Queene,* for Spenser had achieved a national romance of epic greatness in the vernacular, and in the

From *A Map of Misreading.* © 1975 by Oxford University Press, Inc.

service of moral and theological beliefs not far from Milton's own.

The map of misprision charted in chapter 5 [of *A Map of Misreading*], moved between the poles of *illusio*—irony as a figure of speech, or the reaction-formation I have termed *clinamen*—and allusion, particularly as the scheme of transumption or metaleptic reversal that I have named *apophrades* and analogized to the defenses of introjection and projection. As the common root of their names indicates, *illusio* and allusion are curiously related, both being a kind of mockery, rather in the sense intended by the title of Geoffrey Hill's poem on Campanella, that "Men are a mockery of Angels." The history of "allusion" as an English word goes from an initial meaning of "illusion" on to an early Renaissance use as meaning a pun, or wordplay in general. But by the time of Bacon it meant any symbolic likening, whether in allegory, parable, or metaphor, as when in *The Advancement of Learning* poetry is divided into "narrative, representative, and allusive." A fourth meaning, which is still the correct modern one, follows rapidly by the very early seventeenth century, and involves any implied, indirect, or hidden reference. The fifth meaning, still incorrect but bound to establish itself, now equates allusion with direct, overt reference. Since the root meaning is "to play with, mock, jest at," allusion is uneasily allied to words like "ludicrous" and "elusion," as we will remember later.

Thomas McFarland, formidably defending Coleridge against endlessly repetitive charges of plagiarism, has suggested that "plagiarism" ought to be added as a seventh revisionary ratio. Allusion is a comprehensive enough ratio to contain "plagiarism" also under the heading of *apophrades,* which the Lurianic Kabbalists called *gilgul*. Allusion as covert reference became in Milton's control the most powerful and successful figuration that any strong poet has ever employed against his strong precursors.

Milton, who would not sunder spirit from matter, would not let himself be a receiver, object to a subject's influencings. His stance against dualism and influence alike is related to his exaltation of unfallen *pleasure,* his appeal not so much to his reader's senses as to his reader's yearning for the expanded senses of Eden. Precisely here is the center of Milton's own influence upon the Romantics, and here also is why he surpassed them in greatness, since what he could do for himself was the cause of their becoming unable to do the same for themselves. His achievement became at once their starting point, their inspiration, yet also their goad, their torment.

Yet he too had his starting point: Spenser. Spenser was "the soothest shepherd that e'er piped on plains," "sage and serious."

"Milton has acknowledged to me, that Spenser was his original," Dryden testified, but the paternity required no acknowledgment. A darker acknowledgment can be read in Milton's astonishing mistake about Spenser in *Areopagitica,* written more than twenty years before *Paradise Lost* was completed:

> It was from out the rind of one apple tasted, that the knowledge of good and evil, as two twins cleaving together, leaped forth into the world. And perhaps this is that doom which Adam fell into of knowing good and evil, that is to say, of knowing good by evil.
>
> As therefore the state of man now is, what wisdom can there be to choose, what continence to forbear without the knowledge of evil? He that can apprehend and consider vice with all her baits and seeming pleasures, and yet abstain, and yet distinguish, and yet prefer that which is truly better, he is the true warfaring Christian. I cannot praise a fugitive and cloistered virtue, unexercised and unbreathed, that never sallies out and sees her adversary, but slinks out of the race where that immortal garland is to be run for, not without dust and heat. Assuredly we bring not innocence into the world, we bring impurity much rather: that which purifies us is trial, and trial is by what is contrary. That virtue therefore which is but a youngling in the contemplation of evil, and knows not the utmost that vice promises to her followers, and rejects it, is but a blank virtue, not a pure; her whiteness is but an excremental whiteness; which was the reason why our sage and serious poet Spenser, whom I dare be known to think a better teacher than Scotus or Aquinas, describing true temperance under the person of Guyon, brings him in with his palmer through the cave of Mammon and the bower of earthly bliss, that he might see and know, and yet abstain.

Spenser's cave of Mammon is Milton's Hell; far more than the descents to the underworld of Homer and Virgil, more even than Dante's vision, the prefigurement of books 1 and 2 of *Paradise Lost* reverberates in book 2 of *The Faerie Queene*. Against Acrasia's bower, Guyon enjoys the moral guidance of his unfaltering Palmer, but necessarily in Mammon's cave Guyon has to be wholly on his own, even as Adam and Eve must withstand temptation in the absence of the affable Raphael. Guyon stands, though at some cost; Adam and Eve fall, but both the endurance and the failure are independent. Milton's is no ordinary error, no mere lapse in memory, but is itself a powerful misinterpretation of Spenser, and a strong defense against him. For Guyon is not so much Adam's precursor as he is Milton's own, the giant model imitated by the Abdiel of *Paradise Lost*. Milton rewrites Spenser so as to *increase the distance* between his poetic father and himself. St. Augustine identified memory with the father, and we may surmise that a lapse in a memory as preternatural as Milton's is a movement against the father.

Milton's full relation to Spenser is too complex and hidden for any rapid description or analysis to suffice, even for my limited purposes in this book. Here I will venture that Milton's transumptive stance in regard to all his precursors, including Spenser, is founded on Spenser's resourceful and bewildering (even Joycean) way of subsuming his precursors, particularly Virgil, through his labyrinthine syncretism. Spenserian allusiveness has been described by Angus Fletcher as collage: "Collage is parody drawing attention to the *materials* of art and life." Fletcher follows Harry Berger's description of the technique of *conspicuous allusion* in Spenser: "the depiction of stock literary motifs, characters, and genres in a manner which emphasizes their conventionality, displaying at once their debt to and their existence in a conventional climate—classical, medieval, romance, etc.—which is archaic when seen from Spenser's retrospective viewpoint." This allusive collage or conspicuousness is readily assimilated to Spenser's peculiarly metamorphic elegiacism, which becomes the particular legacy of Spenser to all his poetic descendants, from Drayton and Milton down to Yeats and Stevens. For Spenser began that internalization of quest-romance that is or became what we call Romanticism. It is the Colin Clout of Spenser's book 6 who is the father of Milton's "Il Penseroso," and from Milton's visionary stem the later Spenserian transformations of Wordsworth's Solitary, and all of the Solitary's children in the wanderers of Keats, Shelley, Browning, Tennyson, and Yeats until the parodistic climax in Stevens's comedian Crispin. Fletcher, in his study of Spenser, *The Prophetic Moment,* charts this genealogy of introspection, stressing the intervention of Shakespeare between Spenser and Milton, since from Shakespeare Milton learned to contain the Spenserian elegiacism or "prophetic strain" within what Fletcher calls "transcendental forms." In his study of *Comus* as such a form, *The Transcendental Masque,* Fletcher emphasizes the "enclosed vastness" in which Milton, like Shakespeare, allows reverberations of the Spenserian resonance, a poetic diction richly dependent on allusive echoings of precursors. *Comus* abounds in *apophrades,* the return of many poets dead and gone, with Spenser and Shakespeare especially prominent among them. Following Berger and Fletcher, I would call the allusiveness of *Comus* still "conspicuous" and so still Spenserian, still part of the principle of echo. But, with *Paradise Lost,* Miltonic allusion is transformed into a mode of transumption, and poetic tradition is radically altered in consequence.

Fletcher, the most daemonic and inventive of modern allegorists, is again the right guide into the mysteries of *transumptive allusion,* through one of the brilliant footnotes in his early book, *Allegory: The Theory of a Symbolic Mode.* Studying what he calls "difficult ornament" and the transition to modern allegory, Fletcher meditates on Johnson's ambivalence towards Milton's style. In his *Life of Milton,* Johnson observes that "the heat of Milton's mind might be said to sublimate his learning." Hazlitt, a less ambivalent admirer of Milton, asserted that Milton's learning had the effect of intuition. Johnson, though so much more grudging, actually renders the greater homage, for Johnson's own immense hunger of imagination was overmatched by Milton's, as he recognized:

> Whatever be his subject, he never fails to fill the imagination. But his images and descriptions of the scenes or operations of Nature do not seem to be always copied from original form, nor to have the freshness, raciness, and energy of immediate observation. He saw Nature, as Dryden expresses it, *through the spectacles of books;* and on most occasions calls learning to his assistance.

> But he does not confine himself within the limits of rigorous comparison: his great excellence is amplitude, and he expands the adventitious image beyond the dimensions which the occasion required. Thus, comparing the shield of Satan to the orb of the Moon, he crowds the imagination with the discovery of the telescope, and all the wonders which the telescope discovers.

This Johnsonian emphasis upon allusion in Milton inspires Fletcher to compare Miltonic allusion to the trope of transumption or metalepsis, Puttenham's "far-fetcher":

Johnson stresses allusion in Milton: "the spectacles of books" are a means of sublimity, since at every point the reader is led from one scene to an allusive second scene, to a third, and so on. Johnson's Milton has, we might say, a "transumptive" style.

Here is the passage that moved Johnson's observation, *Paradise Lost,* book 1, lines 283–313. Beelzebub has urged Satan to address his fallen legions, who still lie "astounded and amazed" on the lake of fire:

> He scarce had ceas't when the superior Fiend
> Was moving toward the shore; his ponderous shield
> Ethereal temper, massy, large and round,
> Behind him cast; the broad circumference
> Hung on his shoulders like the Moon, whose Orb
> Through Optic Glass the *Tuscan* Artist views
> At Ev'ning from the top of *Fesole,*
> Or in *Valdarno,* to descry new Lands,
> Rivers or Mountains in her spotty Globe.
> His Spear, to equal which the tallest Pine
> Hewn on *Norwegian* hills, to be the Mast
> Of some great Ammiral, were but a wand,
> He walkt with to support uneasy steps
> Over the burning Marl, not like those steps
> On Heaven's Azure, and the torrid Clime
> Smote on him sore besides, vaulted with Fire;
> Nathless he so endur'd, till on the Beach
> Of that inflamed Sea, he stood and call'd
> His Legions, Angel Forms, who lay intrans't
> Thick as Autumnal Leaves that strow the Brooks
> In *Vallombrosa,* where th'*Etrurian* shades
> High overarch't imbow'r; or scatter'd sedge
> Afloat, when with fierce Winds *Orion* arm'd
> Hath vext the Red-Sea Coast, whose waves o'erthrew
> *Busiris* and his *Memphian* Chivalry,
> While with perfidious hatred they pursu'd
> The Sojourners of *Goshen,* who beheld
> From the safe shore thir floating Carcasses
> And broken Chariot Wheels, so thick bestrown
> Abject and lost lay these, covering the Flood,
> Under amazement of thir hideous change.

The transumption of the precursors here is managed by the juxtaposition between the far-fetching of Homer, Virgil, Ovid, Dante,
Tasso, Spenser, the Bible, and the single near-contemporary reference
to Galileo, "the Tuscan artist," and his telescope. Milton's aim is to
make his own belatedness into an earliness, and his tradition's priority
over him into a lateness. The critical question to be asked of this
passage is: why is Johnson's "adventitious image," Galileo and the
telescope, present at all? Johnson, despite his judgment that the image
is extrinsic, implies the right answer: because the expansion of this
apparently extrinsic image crowds the reader's imagination, by giving
Milton the true priority of *interpretation,* the powerful reading that
insists upon its own uniqueness and its own accuracy. Troping upon
his forerunners' tropes, Milton compels us to read as he reads, and to
accept his stance and vision as our origin, his time as true time. His
allusiveness introjects the past, and projects the future, but at the
paradoxical cost of the present, which is not voided but is yielded up
to an experiential darkness, as we will see, to a mingling of wonder
(discovery) and woe (the fallen Church's imprisonment of the discov-
erer). As Frank Kermode remarks, *Paradise Lost* is a wholly contemporary poem, yet surely its sense of the present is necessarily more of loss
than of delight.

Milton's giant simile comparing Satan's shield to the moon alludes
to the shield of Achilles in the *Iliad,* book 19, lines 373–80:

> and caught up the great shield, huge and heavy
> next, and from it the light glimmered far, as from the
>   moon.
> And as when from across water a light shines to mariners
> from a blazing fire, when the fire is burning high in the
>   mountains
> in a desolate steading, as the mariners are carried unwilling
> by storm winds over the fish-swarming sea, far away from
>   their loved ones;
> so the light from the fair elaborate shield of Achilleus
> shot into the high air.
>
> [Lattimore version]

Milton is glancing also at the shield of Radigund in *The Faerie
Queene,* 5.5.3:

> And on her shoulder hung her shield, bedeckt
> Upon the bosse with stones, that shined wide,

> As the faire Moone in her most full aspect,
> That to the Moone it mote be like in each respect.

Radigund, Princess of the Amazons, is dominated by pride and anger, like Achilles. Satan, excelling both in his bad eminence, is seen accurately through the optic glass of the British artist's transumptive vision, even as Galileo sees what no one before him has seen on the moon's surface. Galileo, when visited by Milton (as he tells us in *Areopagitica*), was working while under house arrest by the Inquisition, a condition not wholly unlike Milton's own in the early days of the Restoration. Homer and Spenser emphasize the moonlike brightness and shining of the shields of Achilles and Radigund; Milton emphasizes size, shape, weight as the common feature of Satan's shield and the moon, for Milton's post-Galilean moon is more of a world and less of a light. Milton and Galileo are *late*, yet they see more, and more significantly, than Homer and Spenser, who were *early*. Milton gives his readers the light, yet also the true dimensions and features of reality, even though Milton, like the Tuscan artist, must work on while compassed around by experiential darkness, in a world of woe.

Milton will not stop with his true vision of Satan's shield, but transumes his precursors also in regard to Satan's spear, and to the fallen-leaves aspect of the Satanic host. Satan's spear evokes passages of Homer, Virgil, Ovid, Tasso, and Spenser, allusions transumed by the contemporary reference to a flagship ("ammiral") with its mast made of Norwegian fir. The central allusion is probably to Ovid's vision of the Golden Age (Golding's version, 1, lines 109–16):

> The loftie Pyntree was not hewen from mountaines where it
>   stood,
> In seeking straunge and forren landes to rove upon the
>   flood.
> Men knew none other countries yet, than where themselves
>   did keepe:
> There was no towne enclosed yet, with walles and ditches
>   deepe.
> No horne nor trumpet was in use, no sword nor hemlet
>   worne.
> The worlde was suche, that souldiers helpe might easly be
>   forborne.
> The fertile earth as yet was free, untoucht of spade or
>   plough,
> And yet it yeelded of it selfe of every things inough.

Ovid's emblem of the passage from Golden Age to Iron Age is reduced to "but a wand," for Satan will more truly cause the fall from Golden to Iron. As earlier Satan subsumed Achilles and Radigund, now he contains and metaleptically reverses the Polyphemus of Homer and of Virgil, the Tancredi and Argantes of Tasso, and the proud giant Orgoglio of Spenser:

> a club, or staff, lay there along the fold—
> an olive tree, felled green and left to season
> for Kyklops' hand. And it was like a mast
> a lugger of twenty oars, broad in the beam—
> a deep-sea-going craft—might carry:
> so long, so big around, it seemed.
>> [*Odyssey*, 9.322–27, Fitzgerald version]

>   we saw
> upon a peak the shepherd Polyphemus;
> he lugged his mammoth hulk among the flocks,
> searching along familiar shores—an awful
> misshapen monster, huge, his eyelight lost.
> His steps are steadied by the lopped-off pine
> he grips.
>> [*Aeneid*, 3.660–66; Mandelbaum version, 849–55]

> These sons of Mavors bore, instead of spears,
>   Two knotty masts, which none but they could lift;
> Each foaming steed so fast his master bears,
>   That never beast, bird, shaft, flew half so swift:
> Such was their fury, as when Boreas tears
>   The shatter'd crags from Taurus' northern clift:
> Upon their helms their lances long they brake,
> And up to heav'n flew splinters, sparks, and smoke.
>> [*Jerusalem Delivered*, 6.40; Fairfax version]

> So growen great through arrogant delight
>   Of th'high descent, whereof he was yborne,
>   And through presumption of his matchlesse might,
>   All other powres and knighthood he did scorne.
> Such now he marcheth to this man forlorne,
>   And left to losse: his stalking steps are stayde
>   Upon a snaggy Oke, which he had torne
>   Out of his mothers bowelles, and it made
> His mortall mace, wherewith his foemen he dismayde.
>> [*Faerie Queene*, 1.7.10]

The Wild Men, Polyphemus the Cyclops and the crudely proud
Orgoglio, as well as the Catholic and Circassian champions, Tancredi
and Argantes, all become late and lesser versions of Milton's earlier and
greater Satan. The tree and the mast become interchangeable with the
club, and all three become emblematic of the brutality of Satan as the
Antichrist, the fallen son of God who walks in the darkness of his vain-
glory and perverts nature to the ends of war-by-sea and war-by-land,
Job's Leviathan and Behemoth. Milton's present age is again an experiential darkness—of naval warfare—but his backward glance to Satanic
origins reveals the full truth of which Homer, Virgil, Tasso give only
incomplete reflections. Whether the transumption truly overcomes
Spenser's Orgoglio is more dubious, for he remains nearly as Satanic
as Milton's Satan, except that Satan is more complex and poignant,
being a son of heaven and not, like the gross Orgoglio, a child of
earth.

The third transumption of the passage, the fiction of the leaves, is
surely the subtlest, and the one most worthy of Milton's greatness.
He tropes here on the tropes of Isaiah, Homer, Virgil, and Dante, and
with the Orion allusion on Job and Virgil. The series is capped by the
references to Exodus and Ovid, with the equation of Busiris and Satan.
This movement from fallen leaves to starry influence over storms to
the overwhelming of a tyrannous host is itself a kind of transumption,
as Milton moves from metonymy to metonymy before accomplishing
a final reduction.

Satan's fallen hosts, poignantly still called "angel forms," most
directly allude to a prophetic outcry of Isaiah 34:4:

> And all the host of heaven shall be dissolved, and the heav-
> ens shall be rolled together as a scroll: and all their host shall
> fall down, as the leaf falleth off from the vine, and as a
> falling fig from the fig tree.

Milton is too wary to mark this for transumption; his trope works
upon a series of Homer, Virgil, Dante:

> why ask of my generation?
> As is the generation of leaves, so is that of humanity.
> The wind scatters the leaves on the ground, but the fine timber
> burgeons with leaves again in the season of spring returning.
> So one generation of men will grow while another dies.
>
> [*Iliad*, 6.145–50, Lattimore version]

thick as the leaves that with the early frost
of autumn drop and fall within the forest,
or as the birds that flock along the beaches,
in flight from frenzied seas when the chill season
drives them across the waves to lands of sun.
They stand; each pleads to be the first to cross
the stream; their hands reach out in longing for
the farther shore. But Charon, sullen boatman,
now takes these souls, now those; the rest he leaves;
thrusting them back, he keeps them from the beach.

[*Aeneid,* 6:310–19; Mandelbaum version, 407–16]

But those forlorn and naked souls changed color, their teeth
chattering, as soon as they heard the cruel words. They
cursed God, their parents, the human race, the place, the
time, the seed of their begetting and of their birth. Then,
weeping loudly, all drew to the evil shore that awaits every
man who fears not God. The demon Charon, his eyes like
glowing coals, beckons to them and collects them all, beat-
ing with his oar whoever lingers.

As the leaves fall away in autumn, one after another, till
the bough sees all its spoils upon the ground, so there the
evil seed of Adam: one by one they cast themselves from
that shore at signals, like a bird at its call. Thus they go over
the dark water, and before they have landed on the other
shore, on this side a new throng gathers.

[*Inferno,* 3.100–120, Singleton version]

Homer accepts grim process; Virgil accepts yet plangently laments,
with his unforgettable vision of those who stretch forth their hands out
of love for the farther shore. Dante, lovingly close to Virgil, is more
terrible, since his leaves fall even as the evil seed of Adam falls. Milton
remembers standing, younger and then able to see, in the woods at
Vallombrosa, watching the autumn leaves strew the brooks. His characteristic metonymy of shades for woods allusively puns on Virgil's
and Dante's images of the shades gathering for Charon, and by a
metalepsis carries across Dante and Virgil to their tragic Homeric
origin. Once again, the precursors are projected into belatedness, as
Milton introjects the prophetic source of Isaiah. Leaves fall from trees,
generations of men die, because once one-third of the heavenly host
came falling down. Milton's present time again is experiential loss; he
watches no more autumns, but the optic glass of his art sees fully

what his precursors saw only darkly, or in the vegetable glass of nature.

By a transition to the "scattered sedge" of the Red Sea, Milton calls up Virgil again, compounding two passages on Orion:

> Our prows were pointed there when suddenly,
> rising upon the surge, stormy Orion
> drove us against blind shoals.
>
> > [*Aeneid*, 1.534–36; Mandelbaum version, 753–55]

> > he marks Arcturus,
> the twin Bears and the rainy Hyades,
> Orion armed with gold; and seeing all
> together in the tranquil heavens, loudly
> he signals.
>
> > [*Aeneid*, 3.517–21; Mandelbaum
> > version, 674–78]

Alastair Fowler notes the contrast to the parallel biblical allusions:

> He is wise in heart, and mighty in strength: who hath hardened himself against him, and hath prospered?

> Which alone spreadeth out the heavens, and treadeth upon the waves of the sea.
> > Which maketh Arcturus, Orion, and Pleiades, and the chambers of the south.
>
> > [Job 9:4, 8–9]

> Seek him that maketh the seven stars and Orion, and turneth the shadow of death into the morning, and maketh the day dark with night: that calleth for the waters of the sea, and poureth them out upon the face of the earth: The LORD is his name.
>
> > [Amos 5:8]

In Virgil, Orion rising marks the seasonal onset of storms. In the Bible, Orion and all the stars are put into place as a mere sign-system, demoted from their pagan status as powers. Milton says "hath vexed" to indicate that the sign-system continues in his own day, but he says "o'erthrew" to show that the Satanic stars and the host of Busiris the Pharaoh fell, once for all, Pharaoh being a type of Satan. Virgil, still caught in a vision that held Orion as a potency, is himself again transumed into a sign of error.

I have worked through this passage's allusions in some detail so as to provide one full instance of a transumptive scheme in *Paradise Lost*. Johnson's insight is validated, for the "adventitious image" of the optic glass is shown to be not extrinsic at all, but rather to be the device that "crowds the imagination," compressing or hastening much transumption into a little space. By arranging his precursors in series, Milton figuratively reverses his obligation to them, for his stationing crowds them between the visionary truth of his poem (carefully aligned with biblical truth) and his darkened present (which he shares with Galileo). Transumption murders time, for by troping on a trope, you enforce a state of rhetoricity or word-consciousness, and you negate fallen history. Milton does what Bacon hoped to do; Milton and Galileo become ancients, and Homer, Virgil, Ovid, Dante, Tasso, Spenser become belated moderns. The cost is a loss in the immediacy of the living moment. Milton's meaning is remarkably freed of the burden of anteriority, but only because Milton himself is already one with the future, which he introjects.

It would occupy too many pages to demonstrate another of Milton's transumptive schemes in its largest and therefore most powerful dimensions, but I will outline one, summarizing rather than quoting the text, and citing rather than giving the allusions. My motive is not only to show that the "optic glass" passage is hardly unique in its arrangement, but to analyze more thoroughly Milton's self-awareness of both his war against influence and his use of rhetoricity as a defense. Of many possibilities, book 1, lines 670–798, seems to me the best, for this concluding movement of the epic's initial book has as its hidden subject both the anxiety of influence and an anxiety of morality about the secondariness of any poetic creation, even Milton's own. The passage describes the sudden building, out of the deep, of Pandemonium, the palace of Satan, and ends with the infernal peers sitting there in council.

This sequence works to transume the crucial precursors again—Homer, Virgil, Ovid, and Spenser—but there are triumphant allusions here to Lucretius and Shakespeare also (as Fowler notes). In some sense, the extraordinary and reverberating power of the Pandemonium masque (as John Hollander terms it, likening it to transformation scenes in court masques) depends on its being a continuous and unified allusion to the very idea of poetic tradition, and to the moral problematic of that idea. Metalepsis or transumption can be described as an extended trope with a missing or weakened middle, and for Milton literary tradition is such a trope. The illusionistic sets and complex machinery of the masque transformation scene are emblematic, in the Pandemonium sequence, of the self-deceptions and morally misleading machinery of epic and tragic convention.

Cunningly, Milton starts the sequence with a transumption to the fallen near-present, evoking the royal army in the Civil War as precise analogue to the Satanic army. Mammon leads on the advance party, in an opening allusion to Spenser's Cave of Mammon canto, since both Mammons direct gold-mining operations. With the next major allusion, to the same passage in Ovid's *Metamorphoses* 1 that was evoked in the Galileo sequence, Milton probes the morality of art:

> Let none admire
> That riches grow in Hell; that soil may best
> Deserve the precious bane. And here let those
> Who boast in mortal things, and wond'ring tell
> Of *Babel*, and the works of *Memphian* Kings,
> Learn how thir greatest Monuments of Fame,
> And Strength and Art are easily outdone
> By Spirits reprobate, and in an hour
> What in an age they with incessant toil
> And hands innumerable scarce perform.

Milton presumably would not have termed the *Iliad* or the *Aeneid* "precious bane," yet the force of his condemnation extends to them, and his anxiety necessarily touches his own poem as well. Pandemonium rises in baroque splendor, with a backward allusion to Ovid's Palace of the Sun, also designed by Mulciber (*Metamorphoses* 2, lines 1–4), and with a near-contemporary allusion to St. Peter's at Rome and, according to Fowler, to Bernini's colonnade in the piazza of St. Peter's. Mulciber, archetype not only of Bernini but more darkly of all artists, including epic poets, becomes the center of the sequence:

> Men call'd him *Mulciber*; and how he fell
> From Heav'n, they fabl'd, thrown by angry *Jove*
> Sheer o'er the Crystal Battlements: from Morn
> To Noon he fell, from Noon to dewy Eve,
> A Summer's day; and with the setting Sun
> Dropt from the Zenith like a falling Star,
> On *Lemnos* th'*Ægæan* Isle: thus they relate,
> Erring; for he with this rebellious rout
> Fell long before; nor aught avail'd him now

To have built in Heav'n high Tow'rs; nor did he scape
By all his Engines, but was headlong sent
With his industrious crew to build in hell.

The devastating "Erring" of line 747 is a smack at Homer by way of the *errat* of Lucretius (*De rerum natura*, 1.393, as Fowler notes). The contrast with Homer's passage illuminates the transumptive function of Milton's allusiveness, for Homer's Hephaistos (whose Latin name was Vulcan or Mulciber) gently fables his own downfall:

It is too hard to fight against the Olympian.
There was a time once before now I was minded to help
     you,
and he caught me by the foot and threw me from the magic
     threshold,
and all day long I dropped helpless, and about sunset
I landed in Lemnos.

[*Iliad*, 1.589–93; Lattimore version]

Milton first mocks Homer by over-accentuating the idyllic nature of this fall, and then reverses Homer completely. In the dark present, Mulciber's work is still done when the bad eminence of baroque glory is turned to the purposes of a fallen Church. So, at line 756, Pandemonium is called "the high capital" of Satan, alluding to two lines of Virgil (*Aeneid*, 6.836 and 8.348), but the allusion is qualified by the complex simile of the bees that continues throughout lines 768–75, and which relies on further allusions to *Iliad*, 2.87–90 and *Aeneid*, 2.430–36, where Achaian and Carthaginian heroes respectively are compared to bees. One of the most remarkable of Milton's transumptive returns to present time is then accomplished by an allusion to Shakespeare's *Midsummer Night's Dream*, 2.1.28ff. A "belated peasant" beholds the "Faery Elves" even as we, Milton's readers, see the giant demons shrink in size. Yet *our* belatedness is again redressed by metaleptic reversal, with an allusion to *Aeneid*, 6.451–54, where Aeneas recognizes Dido's "dim shape among the shadows (just as one who either sees or thinks he sees . . . the moon rising)." So the belated peasant "sees, or dreams he sees" the elves, but like Milton we *know* we see the fallen angels metamorphosed from giants into pygmies. The Pandemonium sequence ends with the great conclave of "a thousand demi-gods on golden seats," in clear parody of ecclesiastical assemblies reconvened after the Restoration. As with the opening reference to the advance-party of the royal army, the present is seen as fallen on evil days, but it provides vantage for Milton's enduring vision.

So prevalent throughout the poem is this scheme of allusion that any possibility of inadvertence can be ruled out. Milton's design is wholly definite, and its effect is to reverse literary tradition, at the expense of the presentness of the present. The precursors return in Milton, but only at his will, and they return to be corrected. Perhaps only Shakespeare can be judged Milton's rival in allusive triumph over tradition, yet Shakespeare had no Spenser to subsume, but only a Marlowe, and Shakespeare is less clearly in overt competition with Aeschylus, Sophocles, Euripides than Milton is with Homer, Virgil, Ovid, Dante, Tasso.

Hobbes, in his *Answer to Davenant's Preface* (1650), had subordinated wit to judgment, and so implied also that rhetoric was subordinate to dialectic:

> From knowing much, proceedeth the admirable variety and novelty of metaphors and similitudes, which are not possibly to be lighted on in the compass of a narrow knowledge. And the want whereof compelleth a writer to expressions that are either defaced by time or sullied with vulgar or long use. For the phrases of poesy, as the airs of music, with often hearing become insipid; the reader having no more sense of their force, than our flesh is sensible of the bones that sustain it. As the sense we have of bodies, consisteth in change and variety of impression, so also does the sense of language in the variety and changeable use of words. I mean not in the affectation of words newly brought home from travel, but in new (and withal, significant) translation to our purposes, of those that be already received, and in far fetched (but withal, apt, instructive, and comely) similitudes.

Had Milton deliberately accepted this as challenge, he could have done no more both to fulfill and to refute Hobbes than *Paradise Lost* already does. What Davenant and Cowley could not manage was a complete translation to their own purposes of received rhetoric; but Milton raised such translation to sublimity. In doing so, he also raised rhetoric over dialectic, *contra* Hobbes, for his farfetchedness (Puttenham's term for transumption) gave similitudes the status and function of complex arguments. Milton's wit, his control of rhetoric, was again the exercise of the mind through all her powers, and not a lower faculty subordinate to judgment. Had Hobbes written his *Answer* twenty years later, and after reading *Paradise Lost*, he might have been less confident of the authority of philosophy over poetry.

Echo Schematic

John Hollander

We might dwell for a moment on one of the most famous fragments of broken refrain in our literature, the nonce burden in Keats's "Ode to a Nightingale" following the mention of the "perilous seas in faery lands forlorn" (line 70). The next strophe begins "Forlorn! the very word is like a bell / To toll me back from thee to my sole self!" (lines 71–72). The echoing repetition returns, as has often been observed, another sense of the word *forlorn,* as if some of the perils of the seas lay in the fragility of the vision which they helped compose. The word is, even here, Miltonic, with its resounding of a literal and a figurative meaning. It recalls Adam's sense of life without Eve in Paradise: "To live again in these wild Woods forlorn" (*Paradise Lost* 9.910), where the last word trails away in a cloud of sad prophetic irony: "these wild Woods forlorn" are not the wilderness of fallen nature. Adam thinks he means Eden figuratively, but he is, alas, literally invoking both the fallen world and the lost unfallen one: his trope of the place of loss is an unwittingly literal designation of the loss of place. Keats's "forlorn" is like a very echo from within his text, but it reaches back to another voice behind it.

The scheme of refrain is likewise linked to the echo of affirmation and acknowledgment that we have [elsewhere] already remarked in Hesiod, pastoral tradition, and so forth, in the mythopoeic account of its origination in *Paradise Lost.* The First Hymn (5.153–208) invokes heavenly powers for aid in amplification of its praising voice, even as the Lady invokes Echo's amplification in *Comus.* But the unfallen

From *The Figure of Echo: A Mode of Allusion in Milton and After.* ©1981 by the Regents of the University of California. University of California Press, 1981.

hymn of praise transcends the *anaphora* and catalogue of its precursor Psalm 148 by seeming to generate its refrain—indeed, the very idea of refrain—during the course of its unfolding. Before moving on from echoing schemes to ad hoc tropes of echo, we might examine the Original Refrain in detail.

Adam and Eve (5.147–52) are in Paradise

> to praise
> Thir Maker, in fit strains pronounct or sung
> Unmeditated, such prompt eloquence
> Flow'd from thir lips, in Prose or numerous Verse,
> More tuneable than needed Lute or Harp
> To add more sweetness

—or, as we might continue, to add more of the significance which Schopenhauer felt, and Nietzsche quoted him as feeling, accompanying instrumental music gave to utterance and action. Adam and Eve's language, we are implicitly told, needed no supplementary *ethos* or *pathos,* and certainly none of the *logos* which, for Romantic thought, purely instrumental music came to embody as well.

In this total *a capella* song, classical and unfallen, the original pair first observe—echoing, *sotto voce,* Psalm 19—that even God's "lowest works" declare / Thy goodness beyond thought, and Power Divine" (5.158–59). Then they move into the imperative, hortatory mode of the hymn which follows. They call for the "Sons of Light" to "speak," thus reversing the great pattern of fallen praise (in Pindar's first Pythian Ode, and in the myth of the statue of Memnon) in which light strikes a figurative echo in literal sound from a body, instead of merely casting a shadow: "Thou Sun, of this great World both Eye and Soul, / Acknowledge him thy Greater, sound his praise / In thy eternal course" (5.171–73).

This is the hymn's own primary voice. Its first *Nachklang* is picked up tentatively, across an enjambment which cuts the amplifying echo, the distant *epistrophe,* in half:

> Moon, that now meet'st the orient Sun, now fli'st
> With the first Stars, fixt in thir Orb that flies,
> And yee five other wand'ring Fires that move
> In mystic Dance not without Song, resound
> His praise, who out of Darkness call'd up Light.
>
> (5.175–79)

Adam, who will soon himself call up Sound out of Silence, then establishes the formula / (verb) + "his praise" / in the second half of the significantly varied end-stopped lines that grow into the refrain of the remainder of the hymn:

> Air, and ye Elements of eldest birth
> Of Nature's Womb, that in quaternion run
> Perpetual Circle, multiform, and mix
> And nourish all things, let your ceaseless change
> Vary to our great Maker still new praise.
>
> Ye Mists and Exhalations that now rise
> From Hill or steaming Lake, dusky or grey,
> Till the Sun paint your fleecy skirts with Gold,
> In honor to the World's great Author rise,
> Whether to deck with Clouds th'uncolor'd sky,
> Or wet the thirsty Earth with falling showers,
> Rising or falling still advance his praise.
>
> His praise ye Winds, that from four Quarters blow,
> Breathe soft or loud; and wave your tops, ye Pines,
> With every Plant, in sign of Worship wave.
> Fountains and yee, that warbles as ye flow,
> Melodious murmurs, warbling tune his praise.
>
> Join voices all ye living Souls; ye Birds,
> That singing up to Heaven Gate ascend,
> Bear on your wings and in your notes his praise;
>
> Yee that in Waters glide, and yee that walk
> The Earth, and stately tread, or lowly creep;
> Witness if I be silent, Morn or Even,
> To Hill, or Valley, Fountain or fresh shade
> Made vocal by my Song, and taught his praise.
>
> (5.180–204)

This is not glossed by the narration as "the First Refrain," but such, indeed, it is. Like the famous "cras amet qui numquam amavit, quiquam amavit cras amet" line of the *Pervigilium Veneris* ("tomorrow those who have never loved will love, and those who have will love tomorrow"), the broken echo concludes, and builds up, "stanzas" of various lengths, summing up the essential qualities of the different choral voices. The elements "vary" the praise, as the rest of the hymn will "vary" the refrain. Thus, the "Mists and Exhalations," "Rising or falling still advance his praise" (with an echo of "still" from line 184); then the lovely anadiplosis of line 192, where the winds pick up the motion of the clouds, transmit it to the visible waving of the trees, and complete a traditional symphony of the *locus amoenus* with the warbling of the water's eloquence, followed by the bird song. (A historical origination of literary refrain is to be found in that locus of echo, pastoral tradition. Theocritus's *Idyll* 1 generates a refrain which, in its successive versions, grows self-reflexive: "Begin a country-song, dear Muses, begin to sing" changes to "Begin a country-song, Muses, again begin to sing" and, finally, to "Leave off your country-song, Muses, leave off your singing.")

The final stanza (200–204) returns to the singers themselves. A *tornata* that, like the conclusion of *Lycidas,* frames as well as completes, it is self-referential. Its self-reference is like that of the prayer, which concludes in a kind of caudal or meta-prayer for its own efficacy (and which, in Herbert's poems in *The Temple*, is frequently disposed throughout the main text in a constant figurative undersong). In addition, it invokes the primary world of pastoral. The sounding landscape is "made vocal" by poetry by means of that primary animation which, for Vico, is the "most luminous" of tropes, in that it makes fables of the inanimate by giving "sense and passion" to things, here both embodied in voice. The authenticity of the hymn itself is here avowedly confined to a realm of figure: all that can bear witness to unfallen man's praising voice are the stock fictions of pastoral fable, "taught" his praise. This echoes Virgil's first eclogue, "formosam resonare doces Amaryllida in silvas," even as they are both reechoed, in fallen modulations, in Adam's forlorn cry in book 10 (lines 860–62):

> O Woods, O Fountains, Hillocks, Dales and Bow'rs,
> With other echo late I taught your Shades
> To answer, and resound far other Song.

Adam here is already like Virgil's Tityrus and the "starv'd lover" of book 6, line 769. Even the Original Song is full of echoes, although in *Paradise Lost,* an internal *Nachklang* frequently generates a proleptic *Vorklang,* or preecho. In the poem's pattern of unfallen organization, we must take this hymn to be the true *locus amoenus* (Milton's *locus classicus*) of pastoral echo, and its rhetoric to be that of pastoral praise, not loss.

But perhaps the most remarkable aspect of the scheme of echoing refrain here is that it is employed tropically. The first "echo" of the series which increases, rather than diminishes, in significatory volume is itself a metaphor of the reflection of light. The sun (as Conti says, "author of light to the other stars") "sounds / His praise"; the other heavenly bodies "resound / His praise" in echo, and in conceptual parallel to their return of solar light.

The Original Hymn, then, manifests not only the First Refrain, but the First Echo, (but not the first mocking echo: see *Paradise Lost* book 2, line 789). Even the angelic choir's "sacred Song" in book 3 (lines 372–415) has no refrain, nor indeed any other echoing schemes. It is like sung doctrine, and requires the accompaniment of "Harps ever tun'd, that glittering by thir side / Like Quivers hung"—that is, aside from the shade of pun on "quaver" as musical ornament, harps with strings like the glittering arrows of erotic putti. It concludes with the neoclassical lyric formula "never shall my Harp thy praise / Forget." The only natural acoustical echoes occurring previously in *Paradise Lost* are in the demonic regions of book 2, where they are used in carefully turned figures to describe the nature of damned assent. The fallen angels agreeing with Mammon after his speech produce a sound likened to that of winds stored in hollow rocks, played back later "with hoarse cadence" to "lull" anchored ships (lines 284–90). But we must remember that this concord will only lead to the full disclosure of its own acoustic nature in the transformed hisses later on (book 10). And so, too, with the assent given to Satan's words further on:

> If chance the radiant Sun with farewell sweet
> Extend his ev'ning beam, the fields revive,
> The birds thir notes renew, and bleating herds
> Attest thir joy, that hill and valley rings.
> (2.492–95)

(Here, too, light strikes forth sound, and "herds" half-echo "birds.") But this very simile, his epic need to use it, and its lamentable success in the poem cause Milton to interject, in one of those rare moments of intrusion, his revulsion. In book 4, he cries out "Honor dishonorable" in disgust at the notion that postlapsarian *pudeur* about nudity was present in Paradise. Here in book 2, he cries out: "O shame to men! Devil with Devil damn'd / Firm concord holds, men only disagree." Both this damnable echoing and the unechoing, unfigured music of the heavenly choir in book 3, then, are recalled and transcended in their echoes in the First Hymn. They are cancelled and transformed in a process analogous in Milton to what Hegel calls *Aufhebung.*

The Original Hymn not only originates refrain, but interprets the scheme as a trope of echo—as assent, consent, concert, consonance, approval, and witness. Moreover, its relation to older utterances of the trope is itself resonant. This affirmative aspect of echo's figure completely obliterates a negative, mocking one, which appears in a starkly literal way earlier, again in the demonic milieu of book 2. Sin's account to Satan of her parturition of Death concludes as her son, "he my inbred enemy," "forth issu'd, brandishing his fatal Dart / Made to destroy." The following lines are strongly Ovidian: "I fled, and cri'd out *Death*; / Hell trembl'd at the hideous Name, and sigh'd / From all her Caves, and back resounded *Death*" (2.787–89).

This is an instance of a negation more profound than even the reductive mockery which Milton draws upon, and Sin anticipates for fallen human poetry. She cries out her son's name in a blend of erotic fear and mother love; she names him directly and screams out the general human alarm (as in "Murder!"). Hell's return of the word is the sound of revulsion from caves whose hollowed emptiness has now for the first time been (1) employed as a physical locus of echo, and (2) figuratively identified with negation, nonbeing, and death. And yet the whole event uses the materials of pastoral affirmative echo, perverted in the Satanic mode of eternally twisted tropings. "The forest wide is fitter to resound / The hollow Echo of my carefull cryes" says Spenser's Cuddie in his sestina (*Shepheardes Calender*, "August," lines 159–60), thus importing the hollowness of the nymph's abode into the sound of all the body she has left. But most poetic echoes are far from hollow; rather are they crowded with sound and rebound or, like Milton's echo of "Death," with dialectic. Never again would negative echo resound so immediately and so clearly. In American poetry from Emerson through Whitman, Frost, and Stevens, the seascape or landscape will only be able to utter the word *death* in a barely decipherable whisper.

The comic or satiric echo song depends for its force, then, on the dramatic irony sustained by the primary voice's not "hearing," as it were, the nasty synecdochic echo (else it would surely, we feel, shut up after a couplet or two). An even stronger dramatic irony is generated when the speaker is made inadvertently to echo a prior voice: dramatic form is an implicit echo chamber in this respect. (One has only to think of the role of words like *natural* and *nature* in *King Lear* or *honest* in *Othello,* whose reboundings define the tragic contingencies of those who give them voice. The operation of the trope of dramatic irony in such cases seems dialectical. Is it because of the anterior enunciations of such words that a tragic hero is known to all but himself as an echoer, rather than as a propounder? Or does the classical analysis of the dramatic irony as an inadvertent foreshadowing, an un-self-comprehended prophecy, reveal the more central twisting of the ironic machine?) In the narrative realm, such instances abound in *Paradise Lost.* "Or when we lay," argues Belial, invoking recent pains (2.168–69), "Chain'd on the burning Lake? that sure was worse," unaware that he is echoing the narrator's previous description of the nature of Satan's vastness: "So stretcht out huge in length the Arch-fiend lay / Chain'd on the burning Lake" (1.209–10). The echo, which includes the enjambed "lay," is of a voice Belial has never heard, an epic narrator possessed of some "Foreknowledge absolute." The reader is reminded again how Belial is limited by his ignorance of the script written for him (once he has surrendered his freedom by choosing Satan and the fiction of self-createdness). Even as the modern reader hears a secondary echo, in this and other instances of repeated phrase throughout *Paradise Lost,* of the classical formulaic epithet, he implicitly surveys the distance between fallen angels such as Belial and the Homeric personages who are both his poetic forbears and, in the re-modeled mythological history of *Paradise Lost,* his historical descendants.

In general, when Milton's poem echoes itself, whether from nearby or at a great distance, there is no ironic shift of voice, as in the previous case. In its wordplay, for example, *Paradise Lost* favors the echoing sort, rather than the compact form of the single word: *antanaclasis* rather than strict pun. In the rhetoric of wit, this is usually the weaker form (imagine, for example, "Now is the winter of our discontent / Made glorious summer by this sun of York's / Own son"), where the repetition has the plonking quality of self-glossing in the worst way. In many cases in Shakespeare's sonnets, or in lines like Donne's "When thou hast done, thou hast not done," the antanaclastic repetition embodies a compact pun (so that in order to gloss itself, the line would have to end "thou has not done [Donne]," and it is only the second "done" which is being played upon). It is likely that the excessively unfunny antanaclasis with which Satan sneaks into Paradise, when "in contempt, / At one slight bound high overleap'd all bound / Of Hill or highest Wall" (4.181–82), is mimetically bad—even if Satan's leap is as graceful as that of the winner over the tennis net, the epic voice, in describing it, must change its notes to corny. At such close range, echoing repetition controls the ironies that inhere in the relation of the punning meanings, rather than those dramatic ironies that change of time and place will make literal.

More typical in *Paradise Lost* is the slightly deformed antanaclasis which Abraham Fraunce in *The Arcadian Rhetorike* (1588) reserved for the usual term *paranomasia* (which he also calls "allusion," interestingly enough, from the *ludus* of wordplay): thus Satan in book 1 sneers at the benign rule of the King of Heaven (whom he has just accused of being *tyrannos* rather than *basileus* anyway), who "still his strength conceal'd, / Which tempted our attempt, and wrought our fall" (1.641–42). Milton has given Satan the advertent wordplay here, as Adam is given the gentler and more loving wit, the beautiful and beautifully complex invocation to Eve in book 4 (line 411): "Sole partner and sole part of all these joys." (Here, as Alistair Fowler points out, the two meanings of *sole*—"only" and "unrivalled" are also at work.) But love commands more intricate wit than hate does, and the way in which we are reminded that *part* is part of *partner*—an echo of stem rather than of suffix—is one worthy of George Herbert.

Closely related to Belial's echo of the voice of the narration—indeed, a kind of antitype of it—is Satan's echo of an earlier formula in his speech on Mt. Niphates (4.42–45). At a strange moment of inadvertent admission of a truth about his relation to God that he had previously (and publicly) denied, he avers that

> he deserv'd no such return
> From me, whom he created where I was
> In that bright eminence, and with his good
> Upbraided none

This is the Satan who, enthroned at the beginning of book 2 in a fierce but inauthentic splendor—its description may itself echo Spenser's representation of the throne of Lucifera (*Faerie Queene* 1.4.8)—"exalted sat, by merit rais'd / To that bad eminence" (2.5–6). The memory of the "bright eminence" echoes the reader's earlier apprehension of the bad one, but the dramatic irony is softer here than it was in the case of Belial. An even more poignant echo of the inexorable narrative voice occurs in book 9, where Satan is at one of his most moving moments in the poem.

He has just made his second mistake about Paradise. (The first is in book 4, lines 505–8, where he attributes to the unfallen Adam and Eve, as they make love in a sight to him "hateful" and "tormenting," the necessity for the consolations and errors of fallen eroticism. He says of them that they were "Imparadis't in one another's arms / The happier Eden." Satan is wrong because they are "imparadis't" indeed in Paradise; the notion that an erotic embrace is a bower of bliss is a desperate, lovely fiction of fallen humanity.) A complementary mistake also results from Satan's being smitten with beauty in Paradise: addressing Earth (9.99ff), Satan praises the scene before him, feels the need of rhetorical elevation, then rationalizes the hyperbole: "O Earth, how like to Heav'n, if not preferr'd / More justly, Seat worthier of Gods, as built / With second thoughts, reforming what was old!" Then comes a second order of rationalization: Earth is better because it is the newer model, "For what God after better worse would build?" Again, *le pauvre,* Satan can only respond in fallen human terms of work, enterprise, and progress. It reciprocates for the mistake about love in book 4. From the beauty of Earth and the nobility of its inhabitants ("Growth, Sense, Reason all summ'd up in Man"—a purely humanist notion), Satan moves to the deep pleasure yielded by landscape, pleasure unfallen yet, for humanity or for the seventeenth century, into the declensions of Beautiful, Picturesque, and Sublime, but summing them all up:

> If I could joy in aught, sweet interchange
> Of Hill and Valley, Rivers, Woods and Plains,
> Now Land, now Sea, and Shores with Forest crown'd,
> Rocks, Dens, and Caves; but I in none of these
> Find place or refuge
>
> (9.115–19)

"Rocks, Dens and Caves . . ." Satan finds no refuge in these, and particularly in the dialectic of array and design in pictures and spectacles of them. The reader will remember that the adventurous Drakes and Magellans of Pandemonium in book 2 passed "O'er many a Frozen, many a Fiery Alp, / Rocks, Caves, Lakes, Fens, Bogs, Dens, and shades of Death" (2.620–21). That famous line of monosyllables over which the steps of prosodic theorists have for so long tripped is immediately echoed in the next line, "A Universe of death." Not only is Satan's longing catalogue of the joys of contemplated landscape bound to conclude in the places of retreat and darkness, prefiguring the meaning of shadiness that will eventually become attached to dark places after Adam and Eve first guiltily hide themselves there. He is, moreover, echoing the narration's understanding of the proleptically fallen relation, in book 2's prophetic vision of human culture, of rocks and dens and caves with death.

Adam's reflex of this kind of Satanic echoing—echoing of what has already, and in just those words, been propounded—can be heard in his patently rhetorical antanaclasis at 9.1067. The first words he says to Eve after they awaken, "as from unrest," from their first fallen fucking in a "shady bank, / Thick overhead with verdant roof imbowr'd" (9.1037–38): are "O Eve, in evil hour thou didst give ear / To that false Worm" (9.1067–68). This is the same rhetorical Adam of the "sole partner and sole part," affirming the new fallen phenomenology of Eve's name: it no longer echoes "even," "eve," "evening," but now, as henceforth, "evil." In addition, he, like Satan, is echoing the narration. Less than three hundred lines before, Eve had stretched out her hand "in evil hour / Forth reaching to the Fruit" (9.780–81). Adam speaks almost with a tone of "indeed, Milton was right in saying that it was 'in evil hour' that this occurred," a tinct of wisdom never given to Satan. It is only the poetry of fallen man that will need to employ tropes and fables, similes, echoes, and allusions, in order to represent Truth. We somehow know that Adam is far less mocked by the dramatic irony of the narrative echo than Satan is, tortured ironist though he may be.

The chorus of echoes which accompanies the scenes of loss and regret surrounding the Fall is completed by the narration's own play-back of an already resounding phrase. It occurs in the digression on the nature of the fig leaves with which human nakedness—the fallen form of nudity, ever to require *clothing,* as nudity itself, if concealed, is always to be veiled by visionary *drapery*—first hides itself ("Honor dishonorable!"). The fig tree is associated with a benign primitive role in a Rousseauian nature: the "Indian Herdsman shunning heat / Shelters in cool" (9.1108–9). It is this exotic tree, benevolent and protective in the more exotic and childlike of human cultures, that

> spreads her arms
> Branching so broad and long, that in the ground
> The bended Twigs take root, and Daughters grow
> About the Mother tree, a Pillar'd shade
> High overarch't, and echoing walks between.
>
> (9.1103–7)

Shade in Paradise is a lovely variation from sunlight; this "Pillar'd shade," and that of the "shady bank / Thick overhead with verdant roof imbowr'd" have already been imprinted with the shadowy type of death. In book 1, lines 301–3, the famous and heavily allusive image of the fallen legions of the rebel "Angel Forms" shows them as lying "Thick as autumnal leaves that strow the Brooks / In Vallombrosa, where th' Etrusian shades / *High overarch't* imbower" (my italics). The specific verbal echo accompanies the shadows cast by the earlier text on the futurity of all shady places. And, as elsewhere in Milton, the rhetorical echo calls up the literal acoustical event: "echoing walks between."

There is something like a dramatic irony in a character's inadvertent echo of the narrative voice by which even his own utterance is recounted. There is also, as we have been seeing, a kind of allusive typology in the more possibly self-aware echo of an earlier moment in Miltonic narration by a later one. We might compare these two conditions with the different kinds of irony revealed by the sense of unwitting literalness. In a phrase like Miranda's "O brave new world," the audience recognizes an allusion to a literal hemisphere, of which the speaker is ignorant. Much more like Miltonic allusive irony is Abraham's remark to Isaac, in response to the boy's question about what lamb will be used for the sacrifice. "God will provide his own lamb," replies the Kierkegaardian religious hero; the dramatic irony is again generated by the unwitting literalness of what had been propounded as a trope, here a trope of evasion. But the Christian reading of this episode (not the *akeda* of the Hebrew Bible, but the first figurative sacrifice foreshadowing the trope of Christ as lamb), gives the literalness another dimension. What Abraham offers figuratively, the narrative literalizes when the ram is discovered entangled in the thicket. But the literalization is only a movement into the fullness of antitype: the foreshadowing will be literally fulfilled in the typological completion of the episode in the New Testament when the Lamb of God is finally provided by, and of, him.

It is this kind of dramatic and typological irony that is at work in so many of those highly charged rhetorical moments in *Paradise Lost*. It lurks in the contortions of Statan's manipulations of the literal and the figurative, the local and the general ("Evil be thou my Good" completed by the whining of "All good to me becomes / Bane" in book 9, for example). Indeed, we might learn from the shadows of the unwitting in Satan's rhetoric, and in that of Adam when he echoes Satan in syntax and tone (as in 9.755–75), how central to dramatic irony this question of inadvertent literalness can be. (Kafka's great parable *On Parables* also sheds fierce light on this.) Dramatic irony is often a matter of an utterance striking an unwitting *Vorklang*, as it were, of an eventual echo, of a situation to which it will turn out to have alluded. It might be redefined in terms of manifest rhetorical figuration turning out, horribly, to have been literal. Certainly, Satanic rhetoric provides an origination of this.

One kind of self-echo in Milton occurs in the almost leitmotivic reappearance of phrases and cadences in *Paradise Lost* to which sophisticated critical attention of the past few decades has been so attentive. These form a subclass of their own. As echoes, their voices do not come from afar, or from absent places, so much as from a memory of the poem's own utterance. Their region of origin is usually schematically related to that of the echoic answer: thus, in book 5, the Son sits "Amidst as from a flaming Mount, whose top / Brightness had made invisible" (5.598–99); the reversal of "No light, but rather darkness visible" (1.63) points up the radically different character of the flaming. But such patterns are quite basic to the fabric of *Paradise Lost*, and might be considered as elements in what seems to be the poem's memory of itself.

Eve, Evening, and the Labor of Reading in *Paradise Lost*

Patricia Parker

In book 4 of *Paradise Lost*, in the midst of the description of Eden, Eve, Mother of Mankind, recalls the first moments of her creation:

> That day I oft remember, when from sleep
> I first awaked, and found myself reposed
> Under a shade on flowers, much wondering where
> And what I was, whence thither brought, and how.
> Not distant far from thence a murmuring sound
> Of waters issued from a cave and spread
> Into a liquid plain, then stood unmoved
> Pure as the expanse of heaven; I thither went
> With unexperienced thought, and laid me down
> On the green bank, to look into the clear
> Smooth lake, that to me seemed another sky.
> As I bent down to look, just opposite,
> A shape within the watery gleam appeared
> Bending to look on me, I started back,
> It started back, but pleased I soon returned,
> Pleased it returned as soon with answering looks
> Of sympathy and love; there I had fixed
> Mine eyes till now, and pined with vain desire,
> Had not a voice thus warned me, What thou seest,
> What there thou seest fair creature is thyself,

From *English Literary Renaissance* 9, no. 2 (Spring 1979). © 1979 by *English Literary Renaissance*.

> With thee it came and goes: but follow me,
> And I will bring thee here no shadow stays
> Thy coming, and thy soft embraces, he
> Whose image thou art, him thou shall enjoy
> Inseparably thine, to him shalt bear
> Multitudes like thyself, and thence be called
> Mother of human race.
>
> (4.449–75)

The clearest literary echo of the passage, noted by the earliest commentators, is Ovid's description of Narcissus, the figure whose fate Eve suggests and then avoids, by turning from self-reflection to the acknowledgment of a higher love in Adam, that other "Whose image" she is. But, though the association is only indirectly introduced through the possibility of a pun on "Eve," this moment of self-reflection and turning also recalls that interval of self-reflection or decision which Patristic tradition described as "evening" or "twilight" vision. In puzzling over what Genesis intends when it refers to God's separation of the light from the darkness before the creation of the physical sun, Augustine, and Aquinas after him, explained that in the first, "twilight" interval of angelic existence, some of the angels, perceiving within themselves the image of the Creator, turned from the introspective vision to the reality above them to await the eternal morning of the vision face to face, while others remained within themselves and sank into eternal night. "Evening" within this tradition is the figure for the pivotal, the suspended threshold between light and darkness, which ceases to exist in the final and, for the angels, definitive act of choice.

If indeed, as several commentators suggest, both the Patristic and the Ovidian resonances here coexist, Eve's crucial moment of "staying" or self-reflection recalls the structure of the angelic *cogito*; the suspended or pivotal interval, the movement *intra nos,* may lead either up or down, to that acknowledgment of genuine otherness to which Eve is called by the warning "voice" of her Creator or down into the Narcissistic "shadow" world so vividly recalled in the Ovidian coloring of Milton's lines. Raphael will soon arrive to relate to Adam how the recreant angels fell, and Eve's recounting thus obliquely prefigures both this later narrative and the structure of her own subsequent self-regarding and fall. But here the story is not of a fall but of a turning, and the movement of the faithful angels from "evening" to "morning" vision receives its apt poetic reenactment within Milton's unfallen Edenic hierarchy, "He for God only, she for God in him" (4.299).

That "evening" as the temporal figure for the suspended or pivotal threshold of decision might be present here submerged in the momentary irresolution or "staying" of "Eve" is further suggested by the occurrence of this passage within a complex of Miltonic images and puns which link evening with the persistent theme of the pivot or balance, a complex which begins when Satan first sees in prospect this "pendant world" (2.1052) and culminates in the final event of book 4, the balancing or weighing of Satan's alternatives in the celestial "Scales." It is not by accident that book 4, our first view of Creation after Hell and Heaven, should be virtually the evening or "even-ing" book of *Paradise Lost*. Augustine and Aquinas in their descriptions of "vespertinal" consciousness read "evening" in Genesis as the space of creation, that which is distinct both from the complete knowledge of the Creator and from "night." Like twilight, a temporarily suspended middle, or "short arbiter" (9.50) between light and dark, Eden itself not only literally hangs from Heaven but hangs precariously in the balance as Satan approaches it in the crepuscular or "dubious light" (2.1042) of a kind of "dawn" (2.1037). Both stand between polarities or extremes.

As Satan views it at the beginning of book 4, Eden stands poised between the "full-blazing" (line 29) or "meridian" sun (line 30), a sign of impending judgment, and the regent of Hell who bears "within him" (line 20) the darkness which, in the parody-Exodus and pseudo-Virgilian journey of colonization which brought him to this promised land, threatens again to reclaim it. In the midst of these extremes and the apocalyptic sense of urgency which marks the invocation ("O for that warning voice"), the subsequent movement of the book masterfully enacts the creation, or opening up, of a middle or more temperate space. Satan's apostrophe to the noonday sun ("O thou that with surpassing glory crowned," line 32) seems indeed almost to mark for later contrast the distance between extremes, with a speech whose antitheses and sharp rhetorical turns parody the classical ode not only in its content—praise and petition finally denied—but in its form, the turns of strophe and antistrophe pushed to an extreme and thus to a rhetorical image of the unbridgeable distance between a heavenly power and an unrepentant Hell. Its continual insistence on the polarities of high and low, up and down, raised and fallen ("That bring to my remembrance from what state / I fell, how glorious once above thy sphere," lines 38–39); "high advanced / The lower still I fall, only supreme / In misery," lines 90–92), and the final reversal or substitution in Satan's concluding resolution ("Evil be thou my good," line 110) make all the more refreshing by contrast the sense as we move to the description of Eden of a "shading cool / Interposition" (*Paradise Regained* 3. 221–22) between extremes, of a delicious respite from either Heaven or Hell, "noonday" light or abject darkness. Satan's survey of Eden begins with a description in which, though the glance steadily ascends ("over head up grew / Insuperable highth of loftiest shade," lines 137–38), all sense of extremes or division is muted, all in the ascent graduated or contained in a "view" ("woody theatre / Of stateliest view," lines 141–42) which looks both up and down at once. The masterful simile which introduces Satan's momentary suspension of intent through the "delay" of mariners before the "Sabean odours from the spicy shore / Of Arabie the blest" (lines 159–65) seems to suggest a respite even for Satan himself until the mention of Asmodeus harshly reminds him and us of his mission to conscript this still suspended middle place to the service of one of the two camps.

Images of evening and its delightful suspension enter the book only gradually, first as part of the Edenic mildness and security ("where shepherds pen their flocks at eve," lines 183–87) threatened by "the fiend / Who came their bane" (lines 166–67) and then through the traditional association between the gentler, tempered light of evening and the "embrowning" shade of Eden's cool recess (lines 245–46), which creates a kind of checkered twilight out of the harsher rays of the noonday sun. The first explicit mention of the advent of evening, after Adam and Eve fall to their "supper fruits" (line 331), is significantly accompanied by a pun on its pendency, a play which assimilates this temporal respite to the poised nature of the still "pendant" earth:

> the sun
> Decline was hasting now with prone career
> To the Ocean Isles, and in the ascending scale
> Of heaven the stars that usher evening rose.
> (4.352–55)

"Ascending scale" is a characteristically Miltonic pun, since the "stars that usher evening" must now be rising in Libra, the constellation of the Scales in which Satan's alternatives will be balanced at the end of the book. But the "scale" of heaven also implies the balancing of light and darkness associated with Libra as the equinoctial sign, "Balance bright, / Equall divider of the Day and Night," an appropriate preface to the description of a world which before the fall is not only perpetually equinoctial, but at this particular moment, like evening itself, precariously "in the balance."

We are never allowed in the midst of this pendency to forget utterly—though we are allowed and even invited by the verse to forget temporarily—whose gaze we are seeing this poised and fragile world through, but after Satan departs with his ominous warning ("enjoy, till I return, / Short pleasures, for long woes are to succeed," lines 534–35), what follows is a remarkable series of variations upon the evening, or evensong, theme, as evening itself lengthens out to cover a space of almost three hundred lines. The first of these (the "setting sun" against "the eastern gate of Paradise / Levelled his evening rays," lines 540–43) associates evening with "levelling," as the refractive effect of the earth's atmosphere produces an apparent slowing down or staying of the sun's more precipitous descent. The second ("Thither came Uriel, gliding through the even / On a sun beam," lines 555–56) recalls the earlier combined image of evening both as time of day and as a balancing or suspension of the extremes of light and darkness. Bentley's famous objection to this "even" ("I never heard but here, that evening was a Place or Space to glide through") misses the way in which Milton's evening becomes a kind of "even-ing," a dilated and gradual descent. The image itself for a moment transposes time into space, as the descent of Uriel is softened, graduated, like the gentler light of evening itself.

The "Sun-beam" here looks forward to the punning "beam"—both light and balance—on which Uriel returns (4.590–92), and both prepare not only for the final image of the Scales and its resonance of Miltonic puns on physical and mental "weighing" ("pendulous," "pendant," "pensive," "ponderous"), but also more immediately for the masterfully graduated advent of evening when Uriel, angel of the sun, departs:

> Now came still evening on, and twilight grey
> Had in her sober livery all things clad;
> Silence accompanied, for beast and bird,
> They to their grassy couch, these to their nests
> Were slunk, all but the wakeful nightingale;
> She all night long her amorous descant sung;
> Silence was pleased: now glowed the firmament
> With living sapphires; Hesperus that led

> The starry host, rode brightest, till the moon
> Rising in clouded majesty, at length
> Apparent queen unveiled her peerless light,
> And o'er the dark her silver mantle threw.
>
> (4.598–609)

There is here progression without discontinuity or surprise. The night-ingale "all night long" keeps silence from becoming too absolute, just as the appearance of Hesperus, or the Evening Star, bridges the poten-tial moment of absence or utter darkness between the setting of the sun and the rising of the moon. Evening "evens" the passage from day to night into an orderly succession, or gradual fade-in, of lights. No sharp, epiphanic break intrudes. The movement from lesser to greater light is mantled in a series of graded steps which syntactically almost overlap. The "sober livery" of twilight is followed only by the "silver mantle" of the moon. "Unveiled," with its epiphanic overtones, is balanced by a kind of reveiling, and "apparent" mutes succession and epiphany, heir-apparent and apparent queen, within a gradual ascent.

The moment which for Eve represents a dangerous "staying," a threshold which must be crossed, is here in the very movement of images both dilated and "stayed." G. Wilson Knight singles these lines out from the more doctrinal pressures which elsewhere crowd the poem, as one of its brief respites or more pleasing suspensions (*The Burning Oracle*). But Adam at the vespers in Eden is careful to distin-guish the features of this evening retreat from its more suspect ro-mance analogues and to explain the function of such "staying" within the larger rhythm of night and day, rest and the resumption of "labour" (line 625). Evening is not in his description a static balance or perpet-ual retreat but rather precursor or *mediatrix,* part as in Genesis of the rhythm of creation. When Eve asks about the function of its lesser lights ("But wherefore all night long shine these, for whom / This glorious sight, when sleep hath shut all eyes?" lines 657–58), Adam explains their ministry both as protection from the threat of "total darkness" (lines 665–67) and as preparation for "the sun's more potent ray" (lines 672–73).

The function of evening and of the lights which as it were extend it until day is here again a Miltonic, poetic version of the Augustinian description of the mediate or "evening" vision of the creature, and of that middle space which may lead either down into night or to the dawning whose greater light it figures. Evening, then morning, in

Augustine's commentary is the rhythm of Genesis seen as a figure for the conversion from creation to Creator, from the shadowy, dim speculum of 1 Cor. 13 to the vision of the Sun himself. For those who patiently await the vision face to face, there is no night, but only a period of transition or gradual succession from "evening" to "morning." Evening in Adam's description is both threshold and harbinger, the temporal counterpart of the promise to Eve ("follow me, / And I will bring thee where no *shadow* stays / Thy coming," lines 469–71, emphasis mine). That both lead up, from Eve to Adam's "manly grace" (line 490) and from evening to light, is part of their being still within an unfallen Eden. But this image of evening as preparation for dawn is joined even before the fall by its alternative, a "twilight" vision which leads simply down into "night."

The precarious pendency of evening through book 4 both as a space in time and as a figure for the threshold of choice is made even more striking by the way in which book 5, as it opens, both plays with and curiously inverts the previous book's "even-song." These echoes occur in the recounting by Eve of her troubling dream, a temptation which both recalls the potential Narcissistic moment of self-reflection by the pool and more ominously underlines the possibility of a "fall," a movement from this threshold not up to true vision, enlightening, or "dawning," but down into the very darkness which "Eve" like "evening" stands poised before.

Eve's first words on awakening strengthen the analogy implicit in the earlier scene by the pool between the movement from Eve to Adam and that from evening to dawn, as both Adam and morning are subsumed within single object: "O sole in whom my thoughts find all repose, / My glory, my perfection, glad I see / Thy face, and morn returned" (5.28–30). The passage which follows is remarkable for its anxious repetition of "night" as both dangerous impasse and alternative direction ("for I this night, / Such night till this I never passed," lines 30–31; "offence and trouble, which my mind / Knew never till this irksome night," lines 34–35), but even more so for the subtle twisting of earlier descriptions of evening which begins as Eve recounts her Satan-inspired dream:

> Why sleep'st thou Eve? Now is the pleasant time,
> The cool, the silent, save where silence yields
> To the night-warbling bird, that now awake
> Tunes sweetest his love-laboured song; now reigns

> Full-orbed the moon, and with more pleasing light
> Shadowy sets off the face of things.
>
> (5.38–43)

The passage is so strikingly an echo, or virtual Satanic quotation, of the advent of evening in book 4, with its queenly "moon" (4.606) and "wakeful nightingale" (line 602), that it more than evokes in the reader Adam's later response (5. 114–16: "Some such resemblances methinks I find / Of our last evening's talk, in this thy dream, / But with addition strange"). The "addition strange" which specifically recalls the earlier discussion of evening and perverts it to Eve's own self-regard is the conversion of her questioning of the function of evening lights when none is there to see (4.657–58: "for whom / This glorious sight, when sleep hath shut all eyes?") in the invitation by Satan to the Narcissism of an involuted or purely self-regarding "eve" ("heaven wakes with all his eyes, / Whom to behold but thee," lines 44–45). The echo masterfully conflates both parts of book 4—the explanation of the mediatory function of evening lights and the gaze of Eve at her own image in the pool—in a way which suggests that "eve" may be not benign *mediatrix* but the enclosed limbo or impasse of the *intra nos* or self-regarding vision, and the echo of the conversion of Eve at the pool to the higher vision and presence of Adam to which she is called is here both strengthened and reversed in the line "I rose as at thy call, but *found thee not*" (line 48, emphasis mine). Though Eve here like Eden itself is still "pendant" ("Evil into the mind of god or man / May come and go, so unapproved, and leave / No spot or blame behind"), the sense of the possible proximity of "Eve" to "night" is conveyed syntactically by the characteristically Miltonic juxtaposition which places them in sequence before a new line can undo the link: "Thus Eve her night / Related, and thus Adam answered sad" (lines 93–94).

This darker alternative is picked up in the image which precedes the very narrative of temptation Eve's dream proleptically outlines, as the temporary threshold of evening at the beginning of book 9 echoes once again the Hesperus of book 4 but follows it now only by darkness, a "fall" in which the earlier gradual rhythm is replaced by a precipitate movement from a definitive "sunk" to an already accomplished "had veiled":

> The sun was sunk, and after him the star
> Of Hesperus, whose office is to bring

Twilight upon the earth, short arbiter
Twixt day and night, and now from end to end
Night's hemisphere had veiled the horizon round.

(9.48–52)

What ensues in the temptation and fall of Eve combines all the cumulative echoes of the earlier reflection in the pool, descriptions of evening as "balance," and Eve's evening dream into a *mundus inversus* in which "up" and "down" are confused, in which the fallen Eve, sinking into the darkness prefigured by the literal fall of night (though now at noon), praises the fruit "of divine effect / To open eyes" (9.865–66), and where the half-light is no longer the dimmer lights of evening which prepare for the sun but the "delusive light" of the *ignis fatuus* which leads the "amazed night-wanderer" astray (9.639–42).

After the fall, Adam echoes and reverses his own earlier insistence that the shady bower of Eden and the gentle respite of evening are only timely re-creations in his desire for a permanent hiding-place from both sun and judgment ("where highest woods impenetrable / To star or sunlight, spread their umbrage broad / And brown as evening," 9.1086–88). The literal advent of evening in book 10 as the fallen pair hear and hide from "the voice of the Lord God walking in the garden in the cool of the day" (Gen. 3:8) furthers in Milton the suggestion in the commentary that the lesser light of evening and hiding from God are the same thing. Augustine interprets the "evening" of their sin and hiding as that very turning from Creator to creature which is the basis for all subsequent inversions. And indeed in Milton's poem the fall becomes the occasion for a transformation of earlier images into their parody-doubles. Evening as *mediatrix* or *preparatio* turns in Adam's wish into an impasse or perpetual limbo, just as the fertility of Eve as *Hevah* and the shady mutual "covering" of the prelapsarian paradise have their parodic extension in the fig-tree chosen as covering, shutting out the "heat" (9.1108) of the sun too completely and "Branching so broad and long, that in the ground / The bended twigs take root, and daughters grow / About the mother tree" (9.1104–6).

Side by side with this sense of "evening" as a turning away from "light," however, is the very different sense of evening which enters the poem as the Son in book 10 descends to earth to "temper . . . / Justice with mercy" (lines 77–78), for it is here that a new alignment of the figural ambivalences of evening after the fall begins to take shape. The descent of the Son in this book is accompanied by a description of the descent of the sun, in a passage which both remains faithful to the time-scheme of Gen. 3 and manages subtly to identify the gentle tempered light of evening with the tempering of divine judgment, neither the apocalyptic noon of the *sol iustitiae* nor the time when the sun has gone down upon God's wrath ("The evening cool when he from wrath more cool / Came the mild judge and intercessor both," 10.95–96). The "covering" of Adam and Eve by the Son in book 10 proleptically foreshadows the "covering" of the Incarnation, as event associated by Origen and others with an "evening" which is both the world in its decline and the inauguration of the final "'morning" of history. (Origen, *Homilies on Exodus* 7.8. The *Glossa ordinaria* commentary on Gen. 3 records the tradition that "evening" was the hour of the expulsion of Adam and Eve and of the crucifixion of Christ, hence of both the fall from and the initiated reentry into paradise.)

What had been before the fall an image of the pendency or poised innocence of Eden becomes after the fall a figure for the mediated or the mediatory in yet another sense, the crucial middle or twilight zone of history and of choice, now that final judgment or apocalyptic separation of day and night is deferred or "Removed far off" (10.211). As an image of the "respite" granted by grace (11.254–55), "evening" becomes a figure for that ambivalent space in which the end is both "at hand" and yet delayed, in which pendency is both the "living death" (10.788) that Adam fears and that Eve in her counsel of suicide wants to cut short and yet also a time of turning or "hope." In the submerged Miltonic pun on "Eve," the interval of decision or choice before the pool is also proleptically the mediate or intervening space of time and trial before the final separation of the children of light from the children of darkness, the sixth age of "re-creation" traditionally prefigured by Eve. It is not simply a time when the delightful Miltonic graduations of evening give way to a more melancholy Virgilian strain, but rather an image of graduation in a figural or typological sense, the movement from "shadowy types" to "truth" (12.303). The gospel in the poem's final books is revealed in stages or, as Michael says, in "scenes," a gradual process of enlightenment which incorporates the twilight vision of 1 Cor. 13 into a vision of time itself: "Light after light well used they shall attain, / And to the end persisting, safe arrive" (3.196–97). But again, as in the "twilight" interval of Eve's self-reflection or her troublesome dream, the significance of this threshold depends on where it leads. The uncertainty at the end of Milton's poem as to whether it is evening or morning (the deliberate temporal vagueness of the close, where the "evening mist" (12.629) is posited only in a simile, is striking in a poem which maintains an otherwise precise time scheme) plays yet once more on the crepuscular ambiguity of a threshold which could be prelude to a rise or a fall, "dawning" or simply to a decline into "night."

II

A review of what might be called the "phenomenological thematics" of evening in *Paradise Lost* would hardly be useful in itself except as a way of gauging Milton's sensitivity to the symbolism of times and seasons, if it were not for the fact that the poem itself suggests the extension of the analogy of "twilight" and its ambivalences to the ambiguity of mediation or figuration. The extension of the vespertinal to the figural is already provided for Milton in the tradition of Patristic commentary. Augustine, who is the *De genesi ad litteram* conscripts the rhythm of "evening, then morning" to the structure of conversion and faith, elsewhere extends the vespertinal metaphor to the mediation of the *figura* or "shadowy type" and accuses of indolence those who "linger in the figure" now that the "Light" is come:

> Alas for those who abandon you as leader and who stray in what are but your footprints, who love the signs which you show but not yourself, who forget your meaning, O wisdom, most gracious light of a purified mind! . . . Woe to those who turn away from your light and love to linger in their darkness! It is as if they turned their backs upon you, they are held fast in the shadow cast on them by their works of the flesh, and yet what delights them even there they still receive from the brightness shed by your light. But love of the shadow makes the soul's eye too lazy and weak to endure your sight.

The "staying" of Eve upon her shadow gains from this figural context an even greater resonance: the interval of self-reflection is the threshold not only of decision but of meaning. Adam's explanation to Eve of the preparatory function of evening lights thus moves as well within a tradition in which the "heavens" which declare the glory of God in Psalm 19 are the Apostles of the Word, and Old Testament *figurae* are the stars which prepare for the advent of the Morning Star. The spiritual sloth of lingering or "staying" within the veiled realm of the figure was already by Milton's time a commonplace of exegesis. If Old Testament "figures" were stars which had their ministry to perform as in Adam's description, they were also lesser lights to be eclipsed, like the stars in the "Nativity Ode" which wait patiently for the coming of the Light and then depart, their "evening" the "Morning" of a new birth.

The vespertinal in this tradition was also a figure for mediation or figuration in a larger sense, beyond the particularity of the biblical "type." Milton follows the earliest of Christian writers in extending the dynamic of the "shadowy type"—its dependence at once on continuity and discontinuity, the sense of a higher reality shadowed by, but never synonymous with, any of its "figures"—to the "foreshadowings" of pagan myth, at once bridges to the Truth and dangerous substitutes for it. And the central dynamic of *figura,* approximation and difference, preparation and stumbling block, becomes in *Paradise Lost* the fundamental dialectic of a Christian poetics. If the Narcissistic danger in the figure is that it too, like the shadow Eve contemplates, can "stay" a coming, the task of the prophetic poet is at once to employ and to subvert its staying power. Milton simultaneously builds the lofty rhyme and undermines the potential Babel of figures, and this movement of construction and deconstruction becomes in *Paradise Lost* part of a poetic *Aufhebung* which suggests how the same poet might be at once image-maker and iconoclast.

William G. Madsen explains the phenomenon of Milton's simultaneously building and undermining his own images by suggesting that Milton telescopes the Joachite age of the Son with that of the Spirit, the "intermediary period" of reading and the Word with the end or abolition of all mediation, the "Sabbath" in which *significantia* gives way to *significata*. For Milton, argues Madsen, this passage has already been made in the ascent from "shadowy types to truth." Yet in another sense the decisive passage is still to come. Milton's poem participates in the ambiguity of that twilight interval of time in which, though "figures" like oracles have ceased, figuration remains. And if awareness of this tension necessitates a straining of poetic language beyond itself—a movement from the shadow of the figure to the reality it adumbrates—the flow also potentially moves in the opposite direction, back from the high noon of apocalypse or revelation to the attractive *vestigia* of the poetry itself. The tension is not unlike that already suggested by the poem's images of evening, the difference between "twilight" as theological figure, or even as that combination of image and structural principle Frye calls the "archetype," and the less directed, almost autonomous description of the "twilight grey" (4.598) which Knight felt escaped the epic's more purely theological pressures. The first is figurally directed, a reminder that all twilight states, like the dark mirror of mediation in 1 Corinthians, exist to be superseded. The second, more relaxed, creates, as Bentley however obtusely grasped, a sense of extended space, a place which of itself dilates and lingers.

There are at least two possible perspectives on this ambiguous "middle" space in *Paradise Lost*. In the first, Milton like God puts his people to the test, or text, and their wanderings, or errors, become a necessary part of the exodus from "type" to "Truth." Eve's "staying" upon the shadow in preference for the substance, with its echo of the Augustinian "twilight" consciousness, becomes in this sense a figure for the potentially seductive medium of the poem itself, the crucial "meantime" of reading, a pivotal or pendant zone which, like "evening," could lead either way. Stanley Fish thus approaches the poem's turnings and syntactic feints as part of the dialectics of enlightenment, a process in which error in its ruin leads to truth; in a trial which involves potentially as much risk as the primal scene of temptation, the judgment on readers who do not "come through" may be not unlike that of Augustine on those who "linger in the figure" and never reach the "Light." This perspective makes Milton's poem into what Fish describes as a kind of "scaffolding" which, once erected, falls away: reading, like liturgy, serves to bring the reader to the point where its mediation is no longer needed, to a revelation beyond its scope. What qualifies Fish's argument—his charting of the implications of the reading process to its end—is that this endpoint is finally discontinuous or unknowable. A poem may lead to "revelation," as evening leads to morning, or shadowy type to truth, but the moment of revelation is by definition discontinuous, as in the dynamic of all "figures," beyond the *visibilia* of signs.

A resolutely teleological reading of Milton's poem is finally faithful to only one of its tendencies, a doubleness which may perhaps best be approached through a paradox in which the image, and process, of "evening" most clearly participates, the poem's curious admixture of the gradual and the apocalyptic. The notion of gradual or graduated movement, of procession "by degrees" permeates the poem. Each lower form of unfallen creation, "by gradual scale sublimed" (5.483), participates in the ascent through "various degrees / Of substance" (lines 473–74) from "body" to "spirit" (line 478). The process of angelic digestion, as described by Raphael, "transubstantiates" the "grosser" to the "purer" (line 416), but it differs only "in degree" from the process of mutual nourishment on the lower rungs of the great alimentary chain of nature. The descendental counterpart of the *scala naturae* is the sociable angel's "accommodation" of "spiritual to corporeal forms" (5.573), a condescension which enables man's ascent "by steps" (lines 508–12). The fall, from this perspective, is an attempt to hasten gradual ascent, to circumvent the process of "accommodation" or education by degrees, and to repeat the error of the angel who thought that "one step higher" would set him "highest" (4.50–51) and who enters Eden in one "bound" (4.181). Milton's God virtually equates the space of gradual ascent with the intervening or twilight interval of trial (7.155–61), and it is precisely the attempt to foreshorten this period of patience and "obedience"—to proceed directly to that "Higher degree of life" (9.934)—which breaks the gradual chain of ascent in book 9.

This tension between temporal and apocalyptic extends to the graduated "tempo" of poetry as well. The "acts of God" are "Immediate," but cannot be told without "process of speech" (7.176–78), and this conversion of the instantaneous to the processional also involves some kind of poetic "accommodation." The pun on "due feet" in "Il Penseroso" (line 155) combines the gradual ascent "by steps" and the "measure" of poetry whose "Harmonious numbers" (*Paradise Lost* 3.38) move in time. But there is also in Milton the claim to "unpremeditated verse" (9.24), a claim in sharp contrast to the century's more premeditated poetry of meditation and its reliance on such models as Bernard's *De gradibus*. This coexistence of modes leads to a paradox inherent in the writing of poetry and to a contradiction at the heart of *Paradise Lost*. On the one hand, Milton is the poet of inspiration, opposed to the tyranny of mediation and custom as the temporal accretion of "error" and united with Blake against "Dame Memory and her Siren daughters." On the other hand, he is the poet of "due feet," "measure," and ascent "by steps," of an imagination so graduated that the theologically discontinuous moment of the fall is almost inevitably foreshadowed, the syntagmatic or sequential bias of language almost inevitably suggesting "consequence," the continuous linear chain in which contiguity appears as cause. Poetry as late in the tradition as Milton's epic is almost necessarily mediated, inseparable from the accretions of "error" and the ministrations of "Dame Memory." Memory, in the Augustinian division of the faculties (*De trinitate* 10), is the counterpart of the Father, and Milton's imagination in this sense is Satanic: it does not want to be fathered. But neither is Milton an anabaptist of the imagination. The objection is limited to poetic fathers; no such radical a relation is claimed to his other Source. This difference involves Milton in the paradox of being against the poetic doctrine of "translation"—of the history of epic poetry as a graded series of temporal mediations, the westering of an inspiration from its source—and yet simultaneously for the theological doctrine of "accommodation," of the final disjunction of human words and divine things. In the first, to be mediated is to be secondary, dependent on a chain which extends backward in time. In the second, to be mediated is paradoxically to be initiated in the only way possible into vision, by the descent in divine humility which enables the ascent "by steps" to God.

Because of this tension, it is difficult to decide which is the crucial Miltonic focus, the middle period of suspension, wandering, and trial or the final movement towards resolution and end. The emphasis certainly throughout *Paradise Lost* is on this "pendant" earth, the "well-balanced world on hinges hung" ("Nativity Ode," line 122) to which the poem proceeds and returns. Even the war in heaven, that notorious mythic preempter of the human, is in Milton's epic narrated for the sake of man. The characteristic Miltonic focus is on the process rather than on the product or end. The reader is set before events which have already happened as if they were about to happen, still a matter of choice. And though the action progresses through temptation and fall, the reader remains in a sense still poised on this threshold, before a decision whose coordinates may alter but which still remains "to come."

If we may revert once more to the interval of Eve's staying upon her image in the pool and to the analogy between this pivotal moment of choice and the momentarily suspended images of evening, we may see in the Miltonic fondness for a pendency of image or of syntax the way in which the imagery of "evening" and "balance" receives its "answerable style." Book 4, remarkable for its play upon the middle or threshold state of evening, is also remarkable for a series of images which, like evening, could lead the reader in one of two directions. In the midst of the description of paradise, the reader comes upon one of many provocatively suggestive pagan figures:

>   Not that fair field
> Of Enna, where Proserpine gathering flowers
> Her self a fairer flower by gloomy Dis
> Was gathered, which cost Ceres all that pain
> To seek her through the world; nor that sweet grove
> Of Daphne by Orontes, and the inspired
> Castalian spring, might with this Paradise
> Of Eden strive.

>   (4.268–75)

It is ostensibly a comparison of places—Enna and Eden—but the emphasis shifts inevitably for the reader to a comparison of persons, to Eve as a potential Proserpine. But in coming perhaps too precipitously to this conclusion, and thence perhaps to the assumption of an already "fallen" Eden, the reader must ignore the simile's wider context, the characteristically Miltonic formula of the "greater than." The implication, therefore, must remain poised or twofold. Both possibilities before the fall remain open—the continuity of analogy (as Proserpine, so Eve) or the discontinuity of superiority (as Eden above Enna, so Eve above the fate of that other "flower"). The traditional analogy between Proserpine and Eve is a comparison applied after the fact, but here Eden itself is still "pendant," and the fact that the detail of Ceres's "pain" does not quite complete the analogy may not be so much a weakness in an otherwise impressive homology as an indication of a disjunction within comparison, a potential parting of the ways.

The Proserpine simile is only representative of the provocation which underlies the series of words ("wandering," "wanton," "luxuriant," "error") calculated to elicit in the midst of paradise the "guilty" response. The mind constantly tips the balance, weighing down innocent etymologies with their burdened, postlapsarian meaning. In themselves, however, the words retain a kind of poise, still hovering between the poles of judgment, like the active suspension of evening or the "self-balanced" earth. The point in the simile, as proponents of an already "fallen" Eden have indirectly grasped, is precisely provocation. There is within any framework of analogies a tendency for the reader to jump constantly to conclusions. The mind seems to need resolutions: like Eve after the fall, it often cannot stand the suspense. The reader—like Eve "staying" upon the shadow in the pool or unable to stand the twilight uncertainty of a deferred "doom"—faces two opposed temptations: to linger indefinitely among the signs, or prematurely to precipitate a meaning. Prolepsis or anticipation is the poem's key figure, but it is also potentially a form of predestination, a precipitation of the end before its time.

Milton himself, it is true, often tips the balance, creating a suspension or pendency of meaning only to reprove it as a false surmise, and it is this movement which Fish describes as the exodus through "error" to a final end. Yet, almost as often as this sense of *telos,* or of *eschaton,* is reaffirmed, the desire within the poem for resolution or end appears as a form of temptation or reduction. Satan's admission in book 9 of *Paradise Lost*—"only in destroying I find ease / To my relentless thoughts" (lines 129–30)—and his declaration in *Paradise Regained*—"worst is my port, / My harbor and my ultimate repose" (3.209–10)—join the quest of the fallen angels for the oblivion and extinction of Lethe as movements in which the desire for a definitive ending is only a form of the desire for nonbeing or certain "doom."

Similarly, tipping the balance may be a sign of an already completed fall. It is not Milton but the fallen Adam who introduces the punning connection of "O Eve, in evil hour thou didst give ear / To that false worm" (9.1067–68), the same need for resolution which leads him to etymologize "woman" as "woe to man" (11.632–33). Such verbal reductions are a kind of hermeneutic collapse, the counterpart of the counsel to suicide, for they suggest a way out of the tension of uncertain meaning, a way of making a phenomenon (Eve, woman) absolutely coincident with origin or result (evil or woe). In Dante's *Paradiso,* Satan is the spirit who "fell unripe" because he was unable to wait in patience for the final revelation or "morning" (19.48) of what was as yet only dimly glimpsed. And in Michael's explanation to Adam in book 11 of *Paradise Lost,* "temperance," the opposite both of apocalypse and of unripeness, becomes the means of maturation, the condition of life in the uncertain or twilight medium of time ("So mayst thou live, till like ripe fruit thou drop / Into thy mother's lap, or be with ease / Gathered, not harshly plucked, for death mature," 11.535–37).

The echoes of *Lycidas* in Michael's lines make them a kind of culmination of Miltonic meditations on time, on the relation between waiting and fulfillment. It is part of Adam's despair that his sin does not end with him, but the ambiguous "twilight" in which Adam and Eve wander at the end of the poem is also potentially the threshold of vision, the first step in the process of revelation already figured in Eve's turning from her shadowy image in the pool. The "to come" dimension of the figure is the mark of its insufficiency, but it is also paradoxically its hope, the promise of continued movement rather than the Satanic reduction of meaning, the premature collapse of words and things.

The end of this wandering or twilight interval is explicitly promised and is imaged in the frequent glimpses of Apocalypse in the epic's closing books. Adam before his descent into the vale, and veil, of history is granted a privileged vision of the promised end, of a rest beyond his wandering. This perspective from the end, however, remains a privileged vision and is no more the exclusive perspective of the fallen Adam than it is that of the poem. There persists, if we may revert once more to the Augustinian terms, an "evening" as well as a "morning" vision, the perspective of the creature as well as that of the Creator, and it is upon the implications of this twilight zone for the process of "reading" that we may conclude.

Stanley Fish's analysis of *Paradise Lost* is a resolutely end-directed one, an approach which culminates in his remarks on the "pseudo-simile" as an indication of the poem's role as mere scaffolding, part of a discursive mode of knowing to be superseded and obliterated by the immediacy of revelation. In the example he chooses, the comparison of Satan to the "leviathan" in book 1, the simile is revealed to be a "pseudo-simile" as soon as we realize that "what is offered as an analogy is perceived finally as an identity." Satan is not only *like* leviathan, he *is* Leviathan. Once this identity is revealed, argues Fish,

> the scaffolding of the complete simile remains, but only as a means of marking out an area for the eye to move in. It is an artificial space, with no reference to the physical world of either the observer or of the characters in the plot. . . . Because each simile finds a kind of form within a system and not in its own internal coherence (although many of them have that too), they reach out to one another and join finally in an endless chain of interchangeable significances: Leviathan to Pharaoh to River Dragon to Serpent to Giant to Locusts to bees to pygmies and cranes to imbodied force to sedge to fallen leaves to barbarian hordes and pagan Gods on the one side; Moses, David, Orpheus, Josiah, etc. on the other.
>
> (*Surprised by Sin*)

The "identity" of Satan and Leviathan is, of course, part of an apocalyptic division of biblical imagery, the tendency of metaphor to a radical congruence. But there is something in poetry that will not join a line-up, and the tendency even of this simile in Milton is not necessarily apocalyptic. The Leviathan who is identical with Satan is, so to speak, a creature preempted by pure meaning, and Milton's deliberate inclusion of the leviathan among the creatures in book 7 (lines 412–16) suggests a natural neutrality not unlike that of the serpent before his form is conscripted to a Satanic end. The point of the simile would seem instead to be the crucial space or, if we may call it, "twilight" interval between leviathan and Leviathan, between natural phenomenon and final meaning, as between the "pendant world" and its apocalyptic poles. Fish argues that the tendency of meaning in Milton's epic remains essentially the same: "Correctly interpreted, the icons the visible world presents to us will always have the same meaning no matter what formal configurations surround them." His interpretative principle echoes Augustine's, in the *De doctrina*, the assumption that, when potential interpretations conflict, those must be chosen which lead to the already revealed "end." There always remains in poetry, however, the possibility of hermeneutic leak. The early critics who both praised and blamed Milton for his "digressions" suggest an important insight. Miltonic similes expand as never before the range of analogy beyond an initial point of contact, but they also acquire a life of their own; however interpretively integrated as "homologies," they sing too with a different music. Virtually all of the similes classed by Whaler as "digressive" contain a human observer—the trusting pilot (1.204), the Tuscan artist (1.288), the belated peasant (1.783), the doubting plowman (4.983)—and in each the question of final meaning hangs in the balance. The first extended simile in *Paradise Lost*, the comparison of Satan to the leviathan "haply slumbering on the Norway foam" (1.203), is not only the first feeling in the poem of a "grateful digression," of an expansion of locus or atmosphere beyond the single conflict of Heaven and Hell, but also, long before the "evening" of book 4, the first of the poem's shifts to creation, to a specifically human space. Poetry here creates its own faerie, or twilight zone, and the final recall of the "digression" may seem inevitably a kind of straightening or restricting frame. The mistaken pilot, the gazing Tuscan, and the uncertain plowman linger in our imaginations, long after the comparative "point" is made, as a virtually separable cast of characters, linked of course to the necessity of choosing, and yet allowing us almost to forget that all such allusions to the delight of creation must also be to a fallen one. There is a fullness to the time of these similes which suggests that time's fullness is not simply its "end," which opens up within the poem a kind of inner space, of worlds within worlds.

The movement towards conclusion or end is often present only as a kind of "cadence":

> Natheless he so endured, till on the beach
> Of that inflamed sea, he stood and called
> His legions, angel forms, who lay entranced
> Thick as autumnal leaves that strew the brooks
> In Vallombrosa, where the Etrurian shades
> High overarched imbower; or scattered sedge
> Afloat, when with fierce winds Orion armed
> Hath vexed the Red Sea coast, whose waves o'erthrew
> Busiris and his Memphian chivalry,
> While with perfidious hatred they pursued
> The sojourners of Goshen, who beheld
> From the safe shore their floating carcasses
> And broken chariot wheels.
>
> (1.299–311)

The sequence of tenses in this compound simile is instructive. The first comparison is in the present tense of nature, the falling of the leaves as an annual event. The second is a compound ("hath vexed") or transition, just as the "Red Sea" is syntactically a pivot, appearing first as mere geographical location and only retrospectively as a particular meaning. The third is in the simple past, part of an historical event with an established reference. The movement towards the specificity of the past tense provides an analogy to the movement towards the fixity of a particular meaning, the typology of this moment within the Exodus. But as a whole it remains a movement, an interval in which the crucial focus becomes, so to speak, the process itself. The leaves may recall the fallen souls in Dante, and Vallombrosa suggest a more ominous kind of shady valley; Orion may gain in symbolic resonance from his biblical role as an instrument of judgment. But they are also simply leaves and the name of a wind, just as the Red Sea retains some freedom from its purely typological meaning. The collapse of phenomenon and meaning would be Apocalypse, the end of this twilight space or "pendant world." But there still remains a meantime, and the point of coincidence is not yet.

It may be finally impossible to decide where to place the emphasis in Milton—on the dilation of this twilight zone or on resolute progression to a particular "end," on the delightful or dangerous "staying" of eve or Eve. The even more vexed question of his attraction to the twilight of the "figure" may be finally, like the problem of Milton's "Satanism," answerable only within the realm of speculation. There does remain, however, within the ambivalence of this threshold space a tension which makes *Paradise Lost*—and more specifically its imagery of "evening"—itself a pivotal moment in the history of English poetry. Dwelling on the twilight space of creation or created figure is clearly in Milton part of the lesson of patience, of submission to the discipline of time or temperance, in contrast to the apocalyptic impulse in its Satanic form. But there may also be latent even within this Miltonic twilight both the delight and the despair of subsequent "evening" visions, both a preference for its soothing *chiaro-oscuro* and a species of *melancholia* which includes what might be called a "melancholy of the sign." Gray and Collins celebrate the graduated, gentler light of evening as one of the delights of an *Abendland* or English climate, of a place which, if farther from the sun or "source," yet literally has more latitude. The countless odes to evening which after Milton take their inspiration from "Il Penseroso" and book 4's delightful "Twilight" move, like the "dewy eve" of the Mulciber simile (*Paradise Lost* 1.743), away from polar opposites and the immediate pressures of a decision Either-Or. And Keats's singling out of the softer Miltonic imagination which put the "shading cool / Interposition" of a suspended "vale" in Hell as well as Heaven suggests a Miltonic context for his own delightfully pendant, or "even-ing," visions. But there is also in this post-Miltonic strain a sense of "evening" as decline or distance, of exile both from Light and from final or definitive meaning, an exile which echoes the notes of elegy as well as prophecy in the epic's closing lines.

For the poets after Milton who share the apocalyptic frame of his images, evening is still *mediatrix,* preparation for the brighter light of dawn: in Blake's "To the Evening Star" there is virtually no absence or night, but rather a smooth Augustinian progression from evening to morn. But for poets increasingly less certain of this progression, evening represents a more problematic threshold, its "staying" both a potential limbo and the only refuge from a darker abyss. Eve's vision in the pool has its Romantic descendants in the twilight or suspended interval of self-reflection dwelt upon or within for its own sake, and evening becomes a figure for a limbo or perpetual retreat when the only stage beyond it would seem to be "the mere horror of blank Nought-at-all." The Solitary in Shelley's *Alastor* gazes like Milton's Eve at his own image in a well (lines 469–92, 571ff.) and spends the penultimate moment of his quest in an evening bower (lines 572–645) which finally sinks into death and night. And Keats's *Endymion*, filled with resonantly Miltonic images of evening both as preparation for the dawning of fulfillment and as prelude to darkness, confronts this darker Shelleyan ending before the poem's twilight zone is finally transformed into "day."

The image of "evening" is for poets after Milton an inevitable recall of the lingering twilight of book 4 of *Paradise Lost*, and its power is that it carries with it the stored ambivalence of Milton's more learned and more theological use, even after its exegetical content has been forgotten or misunderstood. Far from shading into "natural description for its own sake" (Griffin, "Milton's Evening"), evening after Milton becomes even more intensely a figure of the figural, part of the larger question of the relation of poetic fable to "Truth." If in *Paradise Lost* the temporal equivalent of the movement "from shadowy types to truth" is the vision of evening as *mediatrix* or harbinger, Coleridge's hope that "Superstition" might with "unconscious hand / Seat Reason on her Throne" ("The Destiny of Nations," lines 87–88) echoes in more anxious accents Adam's description of the mediatory function of evening lights ("earth, made hereby apter to receive / Perfection from the sun's more potent ray," *Paradise Lost* 4.672–73). And even as late as Hopkins and Pater, the Augustinian and Miltonic resonances of "twilight consciousness" are part of reflection on the attractive and dangerous medium of poetry itself.

In Milton's epic, the movement to "morning" separates evening as precursor from its shadow double, evening as perpetual retreat. But there is also—in book 4 and elsewhere—a lingering which resists the pressure of the great absolutes of end or meaning, a twilight space of "creation" in and for itself. Romantic poetry provides us with a perspective by extension on this aspect of *Paradise Lost* and on the relation of the direction of its figural "evening" to the problem of meaning or "reading." And Milton's poem—with its images of pendency, of Eve as creature and "evening" as creaturely—provides us with a revealing context for a poetry in which pendency becomes a threshold forever suspended and Eve's vision a Narcissistic "reflection" which might forever, like the twilight charm of Tennyson's "Hesperides," forestall the coming of "day."

Ithuriel's Spear: History and the Language of Accommodation

John Guillory

> *Thought can as it were fly, it doesn't have to walk. You do not understand
> your own transactions, that is to say you do not have a synoptic view of
> them, and you as it were project your lack of understanding into the idea of a
> medium in which the most astounding things are possible.*
>
> WITTGENSTEIN, *Zettel*

"THIR OWN DIMENSIONS LIKE THEMSELVES"

The simile-allusion concluding book 1 of *Paradise Lost* complicates the
idea of literary history by pushing to a further limit the notion of
reduction, which is the structure of both metonymy and its more
complex successors, transumption. When the simile spends itself, however, there remains something more to be said, and this supplementary
matter is untouched by both the rhetorical reductions taking place
within the lines of verse, and the physical reductions of bodies within
the palace of Pandemonium. I would like to place some pressure on
these additional lines in order to open a pathway from literary history
to history itself, which seems to have been virtually excluded from the
poem but which remains "left over" at precisely those points where
transumptive allusion reaches a zenith of complexity. There are uneasy
currents of contemporary allusion in the final paragraphs of book 1,
ranging from an almost certain reference to St. Peter's Basilica, to
more uncertain allusions to the Barberini pope, and perhaps to the
Long Parliament. These contemporary allusions are inversely related to

From *Poetic Authority: Spenser, Milton, and Literary History*. © 1983 by Columbia
University Press.

the literary allusions; as the past is idealized, the present carries a greater weight of negative judgment. At the least, an air of political and religious decay hangs over this passage, whether or not we care to specify the topical references. The upper echelons of the infernal hierarchy are therefore "unreduced," as power flows away from the lesser devils to be concentrated in a more privileged elite, here an object of Milton's scorn. Within this surprising revelation Milton insinuates an even more difficult notion, which, though it seems at first quite removed from the matter of history, will eventually lead us back to the "native soil" of *Paradise Lost*:

> Thus incorporeal Spirits to smallest forms
> Reduc'd thir shapes immense, and were at large,
> Though without number still amidst the Hall
> Of that infernal Court. But far within
> *And in thir own dimensions like themselves*
> The great Seraphic Lords and Cherubim
> In close recess and secret conclave sat.
>
> (1.789–95)

The line I have italicized is puzzling because we are never told what the dimensions of these devils are. Milton is saying only, "However big they are, that is how big they are." Tautology displays an inherent tendency toward conundrum. Similes of size in book 1, far from clarifying dimensions, permanently confuse them, a fact generally noted. This confusion seems to be their purpose, or at least an intermediate intention. I would like to consider the poet's deliberate lack of specificity about such matters as the size of the devils, an indication of more fundamental difficulties of representational language. The uncertainty noted above seems to be embedded in the language itself, in the non-simile "like themselves." If there can be no similitude without difference, this is not a simile, but the spurious simile does not point to a purely mimetic representation (as though we had been given not a picture but the thing itself). There is still one remove between the absence of simile and the undistorted perception of the devils themselves, and much of the poem is located in this mysterious distance. This much was recognized as long ago as Dr. Johnson, whose formulation of the problem remains perhaps the best and most useful:

> Another inconvenience of Milton's design is, that it requires
> the description of what cannot be described, the agency of

spirits. He saw that immateriality supplied no images, and that he could not show angels acting but by instruments of action; he therefore invested them with form and matter. This, being necessary, was therefore defensible; and he should have secured the consistency of his system, by keeping immateriality out of sight, and enticing his reader to drop it from his thoughts. But he has unhappily perplexed his poetry with his philosophy. His infernal and celestial powers are sometimes pure spirit, and sometimes animated body. When Satan walks with his lance upon the *burning marle*, he has a body; when in his passage between hell and the new world, he is in danger of sinking in the vacuity, and is supported by a gust of rising vapours, he has a body; when he animates the toad, he seems to be mere spirit, that can penetrate matter at pleasure: when he *starts up in his own shape*, he has at least a determined form; and when he is brought before Gabriel, he has a *spear and shield*, which he had the power of hiding in the toad though the arms of the contending angels are evidently material.

(*Life of Milton*)

These objections have a markedly post-Cartesian ring, and the entire statement must be cleared of the charge of anachronism before the substance of Johnson's criticism can be redeemed for contemporary use. If Milton did not distinguish between spirit and matter, except as degrees in a scale of being, there remains a point of divide beyond which *representation* does not reach. The ideological monism can be credited without resolving the dualistic problem at the level of representation. Johnson was particularly fortuitous in his choice of examples, many of which cannot be dismissed as simply illustrative of the more exalted Miltonic monism, or of a supposed Renaissance transcendence of our divided modern consciousness. Milton seems to emphasize this division between spirit and matter precisely where the "philosophy" would demand the blurring of distinctions. Let us take one of Dr. Johnson's examples, Satan at the ear of Eve, "squat like a toad." The phrase does not specify that Satan has actually taken the form of a toad, and Johnson would say that Milton ought to have decided one way or the other; but in fact the uncertainty is resolved in the following lines:

> Him thus intent Ithuriel with his Spear
> Touch'd lightly; for no falsehood can endure

> Touch of Celestial temper, but returns
> Of force to its own likeness: up he starts
> Discover'd and surpris'd. As when a spark
> Lights on a heap of nitrous Powder
>
> . . . .
>
> So started up in his own shape the Fiend.
>
> (4.810–20)

The proper point is surely that Satan's shape-changing has coincided with a trope, and that Milton sees no need to distinguish between the two so long as Ithuriel's spear happens to be around. I would like to elevate this spear to something like a poetic principle and say that it represents an ideal relation between the object and the process of representation. The touching of Satan is recognizably an apotropaic ritual, a warding off of the evil spirit, as well as a translation or revelation of truth. Ithuriel's spear translates, as it were, the simile "like a toad." Although it has become conventional to emphasize the anti-poetic element of Milton's discipline, as though all rhetorical devices were suspect as Satanic, it is just this conclusion which can be avoided by the notion of translation. The simile is undone by Ithuriel, or revealed as literal. The thing we thought we saw is what we really saw; but this is not to say that the first vision was unnecesary. The whole of creation, Milton believes, moves (*translatio*) toward the condition of becoming like itself. This is not an infernal process at all, but one to which Satan is as subject as any other creature. This "becoming" can also be conceived as a paradoxical return, or, within language, as the trope's return to the literal from which it has diverged. Tropes can then be associated with the earlier stage of a progression from one state of being to another.

Readers of Milton, or of Protestant theology, will of course recognize an analogy to the doctrine of typology, whose importance is now fully acknowledged. My own concern is both narrower and broader. Dr. Johnson did not understand that Satan could be either spirit or matter because he did not have Milton's "typological" interpretation of matter itself: from "shadowy types to truth" coincides in *Paradise Lost* with from "Flesh to Spirit." But there is also something very right about Johnson's sense of incongruity because we still do not have a clear picture of Satan, even after he has been transformed into his "own shape." Again we have only the tautology, "he looks like himself." I said that Ithuriel's spear represents an ideal relation and by that I mean to reduce the spear to an emblematic status, an image of a terminal state that is never completed in the poem. The ideal is expressed more abstractly by Raphael in his speech about "subliming" —the distinction between matter and spirit works like a sliding bar in Raphael's scale—but we never manage to see the "thing itself" when we are speaking of "spiritual" beings. This might be a vain quest, after all, and yet Milton worries the notion in every instance where the figurative is allowed to slide into the literal.

I propose to work out an understanding of this process of literalizing in order to assimilate its greatest failure into the achievement of the poem. Ithuriel's spear, we discover, does not always work. Milton touches history itself with this spear, and recoils when nothing happens. This assertion might seem at first perverse, when every reader knows that Milton succeeded so well in submerging contemporary reference beneath an almost opaque layer of literary allusion. The sense of troubled contemporaneity pervading the close of book 1, while it is an undeniable presence, is quite difficult to specify. This is a transformation of sorts, but precisely what does not happen at the touch of Ithuriel's spear, which translates the figurative into the literal, the type into the antitype. History, if it is the medium of the Providential God, is already a language, already a system of figures. The poem ideally restores a more essential "likeness" in a further translation out of the language of historical fact, but the translation ought to produce a less ambiguous picture, a univocal interpretation. This does not at all describe the relation of *Paradise Lost* to its historical context, which is anything but perspicuous. The apparent expelling of history from the poem is a consequence of a prior failure and determines a number of compensatory strategies, for example, the use of epic conventions against the generic premises of epic itself—the poem of national origins. This is not merely to say that Milton is reacting to the failure of the English revolution. The omission of contemporary reference already constitutes a reaction, but oblique reference is not difficult to discover; Christopher Hill enumerates these responses in what he calls "political analogies." Yet the analogies tell us disappointingly little about *Paradise Lost*, which is to say that merely uncovering a "veiled reference" might be a beginning but cannot be an end of criticism. The notion of reaction to failure is more inherently meaningful in that such reactions affect the process of representation where least expected. The most authentic intentions, connoisseurs tell us, are discernible in the minutest of particular details. Milton's largest intentions have to do with the peculiar position he and his nation occupied in a historical process, but all of that "intentionality" seems to have been displaced with the decision not to write a national epic. My supposition is that this burden of meaning has not disappeared from the poem. Rather it has been dispersed throughout, saturating the epic even at the level of individual phrases and rhetorical devices. I will take up first, however, the larger intention, returning to Dr. Johnson's objection because it illuminates, from his very commonsensical perspective, the concept that virtually defines the largest intention of *Paradise Lost*: accommodation.

THE LANGUAGE OF ACCOMMODATION AND GALILEO'S "OPTIC GLASS"

If Dr. Johnson had sought to ground his objection in the language of theology, he would have said that Milton's "confusion of spirit and matter" is an example of an accommodation that concedes too little to the understanding of the poem's auditors. This is to assume the commonplace notion of the doctrine of accommodation, which is basically quite simple: Revelation cannot be expressed except in human language, whose intrinsic limitations prevent an exact description of divine events or personages, hence necessitating figurative or "anthropomorphic" representations. Dr. Johnson could not have known that Milton's understanding of this idea was peculiar in several respects. He did not, for example, believe that the "accommodating" was done by the prophets themselves, who were conventionally supposed to have had a vision of naked truth. Rather the accommodating was done by the divine mediator speaking to the prophets. Nor did Milton believe that the language of the Bible need be historically accommodated, that is, adjusted to the understanding of a reader's particular time or place. Johnson's remarks, in focusing upon the problem of spirit and matter as a question of representation, imply that Milton ought to have accommodated the language of the Bible just as this language had earlier accommodated the vision of the prophets. We are better able, it would seem, to conceive of immateriality than to accept the too physically weighted depiction of Miltonic angels. To Johnson, Milton's representation seems strangely archaic. In truth, Milton's hermeneutic was by the standards of his own time remarkably enlightened. He applied to the Bible a principle that H. R. McCallum, his best interpreter on this subject, calls Kantian. Here is *De Doctrina* on the representation of God:

> Our safest way is to form in our minds such a conception of God, as shall correspond with his own delineation and representation of himself in the sacred writings. For granting

that both in the literal and figurative descriptions of God, he is exhibited not as he really is, but in such a manner as may be within the scope of our comprehensions, yet we ought to entertain such a conception of him, as he, in condescending to accommodate himself to our capacities, has shewn that he desires we should conceive. For it is on this very account that he has lowered himself to our level, lest in our flights above the reach of human understanding, and beyond the written work of Scripture, we should be tempted to indulge in vague cogitations and subtleties.

Several extraordinary conclusions follow from so radical a statement, the most obvious being the flattening out of biblical language: it no longer makes sense to distinguish between the literal and the figurative, since no literal basis can be specified for any figurative depiction of deity. It should be evident already that such a doctrine will have a huge effect upon the status of figurative discourse in *Paradise Lost*, lending impetus to what might be called the literal drift of Milton's tropes. A second, "Kantian" conclusion is determined by the "noumenal" status given to God in this argument. The language of the Bible expresses as much as we can know of God; our understanding is therefore limited by language itself. A third conclusion touches upon the status of the poet in a poem aspiring to the condition of the sacred text, and reintroduces into this larger context all of the problems of authority and inspiration structuring this essay.

If indeed the Muse responds to the gesture of invocation, as Milton evidently believed, this would have to mean that the language of *Paradise Lost* is *already accommodated*, and that Milton's own intentions can only coincide with, not precede or succeed, the intentions of the "superior power" speaking through him. When we speak of intentions, then, under the rubric of accommodation, it follows that the intentions of the poet are qualified out of existence. There is no sense in which the poet can be said to have intentions, since that would imply at the least some accommodation on his part. The oddity of such a stance demands an equally unusual interpretive posture, even something of a contortion, because we feel that the poem can only be an intentional act, and that this act is really Milton's. Let me offer as an example of how this problem has affected criticism, the difference between two very fine critics of *Paradise Lost*, William Madsen and William Kerrigan. First Madsen, whose text is the passage from *De Doctrina* quoted above:

Here and here only Milton refuses to conceptualize the figurative language of the Bible, and in this respect (it may be
added) he is almost alone among his Protestant contemporaries. In interpreting biblical passages that do not refer to
God Himself, however, Milton consistently distrusts metaphorical statements of doctrine and seeks to go behind them
by referring to other, literal statements, even in passages
referring to Christ and the sacraments. It is therefore difficult to understand what it means to say that Milton uses the
method of accommodation in *Paradise Lost*, since he would
hardly arrogate to himself a mode of understanding and
expression that he denies to the human authors of the Bible
and reserves to God alone. He of course uses the biblical
language by which God has accommodated Himself to our
understandings, but this does not make him a Moses who
has "looked on the face of truth unveiled." Nor does the
fact that Raphael, as a fictional character, tells Adam that he
must use the method of accommodation in describing the
War in Heaven mean that Milton thought that he himself
was in possession of truths so ineffable that he had to "accommodate" them to ordinary human understanding by
veiling them in myth and allegory. As a fictional character
the narrator does indeed lay claim to such knowledge, but
unless we are willing to grant that John Milton was literally
inspired, there seems to be no meaningful way to relate this
fictional claim to the language of *Paradise Lost*.

(*From Shadowy Types to Truth*)

Madsen is disputing here and throughout his study a Neoplatonic view
of Miltonic representation, and on this point he is on safe ground.
There is no evidence that Milton is accommodating an ineffable visionary experience; this style of mysticism is incompatible with what we
know of both his theological allegiances and his character. The logic of
Madsen's argument is virtually hermetic until the final sentence, when
the troublesome notion of "literal inspiration" enters the discussion as
a foreign element, a term belonging to a different category of discourse. Surely the validity of the argument ought not to be contingent
upon our discrediting the literality of Milton's inspiration? Madsen
goes on to stress the fictionality of the poem, which leads to the
conclusion that Milton is writing exegetically, not in the manner of
scripture itself but of scriptural interpretation. For Madsen this means

typologically, where the intention of retelling a biblical story implies the elucidation of antitypes. I am inclined to accept the construing of Milton's "figurative" intentions as typological, but I am by no means assured that Milton himself always equated a type with a figure of speech. Tropes in the Bible, as Madsen himself reminds us, were set apart by Milton (he "distrusts metaphorical statements and seeks to go behind them to other, literal statements"), in contradistinction to types, which define a relation between literal events. In short, a type can only be considered a trope from a certain point of view, and we have not as yet determined where Milton stands in the reading of types. In this light, let us consider Kerrigan's comment on Madsen's paragraph:

> I can find no place in the poem where the narrator "does indeed lay claim" to knowledge that he cannot communicate to the reader. There is only one accommodation in the epic: the Muse accommodates divine truth for the narrator, who then transcribes this accommodation for the reader. Both poet and reader are spectators at the heavenly court. Aside from this defect, Madsen seems to emerge victorious.
>
> (*The Prophetic Milton*)

Again a question of the reader's belief seems to affect radically the object of representation, where every canon of readerly objectivity argues against this confusion. I have already tried to demonstrate how deliberately Milton seeks to evade tropes in representing himself at the moment of inspiration, but as yet a larger question of intention remains unanswered. Why does the writer of *Paradise Lost* need to be inspired if he only repeats or reinterprets the matter of the Bible? Both Madsen and Kerrigan seem to be arguing against any Miltonic intention to accommodate divine truth, although both positions, as critical postures, are involved in an inexplicable difficulty of language. I want to suggest an analogy here between the idea of accommodation and a reflection by Ludwig Wittgenstein on the subject of "intention":

> By "intention" I mean here what uses a sign in a thought. The intention seems to interpret, to give the final interpretation; which is not a further sign or picture, but something else—the thing that cannot be further interpreted. But what we have reached is a psychological, not a logical terminus.
>
> Think of a sign language, an "abstract" one, I mean one that is strange to us, in which we do not feel at home, in which, as we should say, we do not *think*; and let us imagine

this language interpreted by a translation into—as we should like to say—an unambiguous picture-language, a language consisting of pictures painted in perspective. It is quite clear that it is much easier to imagine different *interpretations* of the written language than of a picture painted in the usual way. Here we shall also be inclined to think that there is no further possibility of interpretation.

(Zettel)

Insofar as the idea of "accommodation" implies the difficulty of comprehending the matter being accommodated, we can say that the theological problem recapitulates the linguistic situation of relating intention (here, Wittgenstein's "strange" language) to the accommodation (here, the "picture language"). When we discuss the notions of accommodation and inspiration in Milton, we experience something of the futility of guessing at intentions. At the same time, as Wittgenstein very cannily observes, interpretation makes just this claim: to have guessed rightly about intentions and hence "rested" (in a psychological sense). We demand further of interpretive language that it be reductive, that it give us the "unambiguous picture language," which in turn recapitulates the linguistic situation of the translation of tropes into original literal significations. This would coincide in my own argument with the touch of Ithuriel's spear. I do not believe that any interpretation can free itself from the tangles of intentionality, and I find it possible to move past Madsen and Kerrigan's dilemma only by making a further "guess" about Milton's intentions.

Milton's predisposition to deny having intentions is evident from the very first lines of the poem, where the subject of "intends to soar" is not "I" but "song":

> I thence
> Invoke thy aid to my advent'rous Song,
> That with no middle flight intends to soar
> Above th'Aonian Mount.

Of course we remember these lines as an expression of personal intention, even though the grammatical evasion is a consistent feature of Miltonic invocation. Milton intends only the intermediacy of his act, and the ultimate intention, the "meaning," belongs to the ultimate intender, the Muse. The one easily identifiable intention—the self-effacing of the ego in the act of invocation—ought to result in the kind of text Milton would have believed to be sacred. To that extent,

Kerrigan's argument ought to be credited. But if the idea of accommodation implies the noumenal status of divine intention, the concept itself becomes almost superfluous. We cannot interpret at all where intentions are asserted to be unknowable. It is typical of both Milton and radical Protestant theologians that they deny interpreting the Bible, which is supposed to be the one text that means exactly what it says. The sacred text seems to have a double nature as both accommodated, and therefore possessing a secret meaning, and utterly perspicuous. When the reader of Milton's epic declines to read the poem as scripture (Kerrigan reads Milton *programatically* as scripture), a host of specifically personal intentions, ranging from a desire for literary fame to the possibility of reaction to the failure of the English revolution, reenter the poem. These intentions are not compatible with the primary intention of acting only as the inspired agent, the voice of the "superior power." Critics will at this point (though they have not yet analyzed this moment of choice) throw out one set of intentions or the other (Kerrigan's inspirationalism versus Madsen's anti-inspirationalism), or falsely reconcile conflicting elements by resorting to a hypothetical "unconscious intention" (Tillyard, Hyman, Empson).

To the question, does Milton write *Paradise Lost* for reasons not explicit in either the subject, genre, or the personal statements of invocation, the answer would have to be, yes. Recovering the inexplicit intention, however, has proven to be a game without rules, or rather, a haphazard "accommodation" of the language of *Paradise Lost* by literary exegetes. It is more important at this point to acknowledge the confusion pervading discussion of this issue, than to clarify the notion of intentionality, which is beyond the scope of this, or perhaps any, essay. All that we can say, with Wittgenstein, is that the interpretation which is an "unambiguous picture language" remains unavailable to us. It is only an idea, like the unimaginable image of Satan touched by Ithuriel's spear, or the face of God. The problem of accommodation is a persistent concern for Milton the poet, because it expresses the effort to represent both "things invisible to mortal sight" and things which are too visible, but which have disappeared behind the surface of the poem: the matter of history itself. The two problems, of divine intention and of historical circumstances, are therefore both expressed in the poem as the *single* problem of representing the invisible. In order now to "see" how these two problems are conflated, we shall need not Ithuriel's spear, but an instrument of human vision, the "optic glass" of Galileo.

My developing "guess" about Milton's intentions is founded in part upon the curious circumstance that Galileo happens to be the only contemporary name, or overt topical reference, in *Paradise Lost*. If contemporary history is related to what critics have regarded as "unconscious intention" in the poem, then the appearance of Galileo might be considered a return of the repressed, Milton's failure to keep history wholly purged from his redaction of the biblical story, which is intended, after all, to tell us what *precedes* history. This hypothesis is worth considering, tentatively, because it highlights so conspicuously the absence of contemporary reference. A more complete absence might have gone unnoticed, which is to say that the return of the repressed is the only evidence of the presence which is also an absence: the repressed content. In a moment, we shall be able to discard the notion of repressing as not entirely adequate. Galileo makes his way into the poem initially through the front door; Milton seems to believe that it is safe to bring him in. This first mention concerns the shield of Satan:

> his ponderous shield
> Ethereal temper, massy, large and round,
> Behind him cast; the broad circumference
> Hung on his shoulders like the Moon, whose Orb
> Through Optic Glass the Tuscan Artist views
> At Ev'ning from the top of Fesole,
> Or in Valdarno, to descry new Lands,
> Rivers or Mountains in her spotty Globe.
>
> (1.284–91)

Although we learn later that this particular aid to vision is limited in efficiency, there is something in Milton's metaphysics that might lead us to wonder, if only momentarily, whether a powerful enough telescope could bring heaven itself before our eyes. That is, so long as we believe heaven to be a place. Among its contemporaries the telescope seemed to provoke a great anxiety; it signified forbidden knowledge and forbidden aspirations, a more intellectualized version of the Tower of Babel. What is the relation between this kind of augmented vision, and the "vision" of inspiration? Possibly Milton had worked this problem through in the invocation to book 3, but at the expense of reinstating the distinction between a corporeal and spiritual sight, of fixing the bar where ideally it should slide up and down. When Raphael (Milton's *Siderius Nuncius*, more authoritative than Galileo's) argues for the necessity of accommodation in relating the war in heaven, he too is compelled to reinstate this boundary, but not without two interesting qualifications:

> how last unfold
> The secrets of another World, perhaps
> Not lawful to reveal? yet for thy good
> This is dispenst, and what surmounts the reach
> Of human sense, I shall delineate so,
> By lik'ning spiritual to corporal forms,
> As may express them best, though what if Earth
> Be but the shadow of Heav'n, and things therein
> Each to other like more than on Earth is thought?
> (5.568–76)

If there is an analogy in Milton's language between the telescope and the method of accommodation, a similar anxiety attaches to both. The descending movement of accommodation corresponds to, or passes along the way, the ascending "reach" of human vision, and at the place of coincidence, a doubt arises. Leslie Brisman suggests that the voice we hear in these lines is more Milton's own than elsewhere in Raphael's speech; for a moment the anxiety is great enough to force the poet into speaking *in propria persona*. If Milton is truly compelled by his understanding of accommodation to deny his own initiation of this process, then it follows that he can no more know what Raphael is "translating" into human language than his readers; and this is difficult to believe. The introduction of typology in the last lines of the passage answers the doubt about the "lawfulness" of this translation by permitting the distinction between corporeal (earthly) and spiritual (heavenly) to fade. The narrator need not claim a visionary experience, nor need he be defended for revealing secrets "not lawful."

Nevertheless an element of uncertainty remains. The same uncertainty is intimated in the first reference to Galileo, not so much in defects of vision attributable to the telescope as in the object whose true nature is being revealed: the moon. The notion of "new Lands" recurs in the voyaging of Satan and Raphael, always attended with a measure of uncertainty. And of course the moon itself is an image of both instability and (as in Spenser) the threshold between two orders of reality. The telescope reveals, as it were, uncertainty itself. With each succeeding appearance of Galileo, this focus on the lack of focus evolves into the thematization of cosmological uncertainty. Satan travels in book 3 through the "calm Firmament; but up or down / By centre or eccentric hard to tell." This line is taken by editors to indicate Milton's hesitation between Ptolemaic and Copernican systems, but I read this hesitation as the sign of a much greater doubt. Knowledge of local astronomy seems a rather trivial secret to keep after revelations of war in heaven, and it is more likely that the uncertainty attending the latter is transferred to a less sensitive area. At any rate, in the next few lines Milton is striving to assert the priority of his accommodated text to the discoveries of the telescope, as though the method of transumption were needed to preempt Galileo:

> There lands the Fiend, a spot like which perhaps
> Astronomer in the Sun's lucent Orb
> Through his glazed Optic Tube yet never saw.
>
> (3.588–90)

Galileo has not, nor can he ever, see what we are seeing here. The discovery of sunspots is transformed into another myth of Satanic origin, an ironic deflation of what Milton's editor calls "one of the most exciting astronomical events of the century."

The last, and perhaps the most interesting, mention of Galileo (this time, by name) forms part of an elaborate description of Raphael's descent to Earth, and with these lines, there is no longer any question of Milton's resistance to the meaning the telescope is beginning to possess:

> From hence, no cloud, or, to obstruct his sight,
> Star interpos'd, however small he sees,
> Not unconform to other shining Globes,
> Earth and the Gard'n of God, with Cedars crown'd
> Above all Hills. As when by night the Glass
> Of Galileo, less assur'd observes
> Imagin'd Lands and Regions in the Moon.
>
> (5.257–63)

Raphael's vision, as the reader expects, can only be more accurate than Galileo's, but the point of interest is that the problem of accommodation has finally, very explicitly, intersected with the upward aspiration of human vision. This is the great accommodative moment in the poem, when divinity condescends to explain its intentions to the limited reason of man. The limitation which makes this condescension necessary is then associated with the defects of even the augmented vision of Galileo, who is first slighted ("less assur'd") and whose discovery of "new Lands" in book 1 is then glossed as "imagin'd Lands." Geoffrey Hartman has commented on the way in which the idea of accommodation is worked into the description of Raphael's wings, which "shade / His lineaments divine," figuring in that "shadow" the "self-veiling nature of divine light." This is as perfect an emblem of accommodative representation as Milton conceived, and within the emblematic portrait Raphael can move freely from the shape (representation) of a phoenix ("to all the Fowles he seems / A phoenix") to his "proper shape" as a winged seraph. The impacted image allows the fusion of literal and figurative to stand for the much more desired effacing of the boundary between heaven and earth. Ithuriel's spear is at such moments an internalized principle of representation.

There is also an analogy in these lines to the psychological terms Milton worked so hard to keep apart: If inspiration is associated with the method of accommodation, then imagination is inevitably linked to the failure of the method, or anxiety about the possibility of failure. The "imagin'd" is once more devalued and set against the authority of inspiration, the non-usurping *nuncius*. When Raphael worries about the possibility of usurping the authority whose message he is delivering, he casts himself momentarily in the role of imagination as it was conceived by Bacon or Hobbes. But the moment passes. The major anxiety continues to be projected onto Galileo, whose "imagin'd Lands" hint at the distortion of imagination itself. Galileo emerges as one of the more overdetermined figures in the poem, carrying with him a burden of meaning deeply involved in Milton's complex theologico-poetic.

If it was inevitable, then, according to the inner logic of this system, that Raphael and Galileo should be brought together, the significance of their juxtaposition is even more extensive than has yet been indicated. I have suppressed, of course, the personal significance of Galileo, whose name is often read as a metonymic signature for John Milton. Certainly his status as blind prisoner of the Inquisition is initially responsible for his safe entry into the poem, though not for his involvement in the representational problems of the accommodated text. The latter development has more to do with the meaning Milton has already given to Galileo in the pages of *Areopagitica*, and which he is evidently remembering in *Paradise Lost*:

> There it was that I found and visited the famous Galileo,
> grown old, a prisoner of the Inquisition for thinking in

> astronomy otherwise than the Franciscan and Dominican
> licencers thought. And though I knew that England then
> was groaning loudest under the prelatical yoke, nevertheless
> I took it as a pledge of future happiness that other nations
> were so persuaded of her liberty.

If Milton did remember the context of the earlier passage, that memory must inevitably have suggested to him an unwelcome pattern of
repetition. His identification with Galileo is only possible because the
"pledge of future happiness" was not fulfilled. The Inquisition is a
principle of historical repetition over which revolution has not tri-
umphed. The resonance of identification is easy to detect, and we are
in a position now to understand what this resonance means: history
and accommodation share a repetitional structure denied alike by both
the Galilean discovery of "new Lands" and the promise of revolution,
a new earth, if not a new heaven.

THE THIRD TEMPLE

To insist longer upon the "already accommodated" text of *Paradise Lost* would be to surrender the poem to an evasive theological
concept, to read it as though it were a sacred text. The method of
accommodation translates intentionality into theological language by
transferring intention itself to the mind of divinity, and this method
can be used equally for "things invisible to mortal sight" and things
purged from the poem's field of reference—the matter of history. Both
are *things not seen*. And this is why Kerrigan's reading of Milton as
scripture effectively de-historicizes the poem, as does Joseph Wittreich's,
whose prophetic Milton also denies repetition in history: "For Milton,
it is not especially important that history repeats itself but that, as
Mark Twain once wrote, it rhymes, and through its rhymes holds out
the possibility of progress." This might have been true for Milton in
the 1640s but not for the poet of *Paradise Lost*. In reacting now against
the current and very valuable conception of the "prophetic" Milton, I
would also want to avoid the opposite error of hypothesizing an
"unconscious intention," which restores Milton to history by evading
the explicit intentions altogether. For that reason, I do not consider the
figure of Galileo so much a return of the repressed as a cryptic self-
portrait. The Milton who accommodates his poem to the vast failure
which is historical repetition knowingly conceals this accommodation.
The concealment itself is only covertly admitted in the negative reflec-

tion of acommodation in Galileo's glass. The hiddenness of Milton's meaning need not be considered bad faith; I am more impressed by Milton's painful honesty in dwelling at length upon difficult subjects. I refer instead to Angus Fletcher's remark that Milton "could not afford the Shakespearean openness," and that the "burying" of his meanings was necessitated by the very age in which he lived. It is possible now to explain why this is so.

Let me begin with an image drawn from an early text on the theme of historical repetition, from book 1, chapter 2, of *The Reason of Church Government*:

> As therefore it is unsound to say that God hath not appointed any set government in his Church, so is it untrue. Of the time of the Law there can be no doubt; for to let passe the institution of Priests and Levites, which is too cleare to be insisted upon, which the Temple came to be built, which in plaine judgement could breed no essential change either in religion, or in the Priestly government; yet God to shew how little he could endure that men should be tampring and contriving in his worship, though in things of lesse regard, gave to *David* for *Solomon* not only a pattern and modell of the Temple, but a direction for the courses of the Priests and Levites, and for all the worke of their service. At the returne from the Captivity things were only restor'd after the ordinance of *Moses* and *David*; or if the least alteration be to be found, they had with them inspired men, Prophets, and it were not sober to say they did ought of moment without divine intimation. In the Prophesie of *Ezekiel* from the 40 Chapt. onward, after the destruction of the Temple, God by his Prophet seeking to weane the hearts of the Jewes from their old law to expect a new and more perfect reformation under Christ, sets out before their eyes the stately fabrick & constitution of his Church, with al the ecclesiasticall functions appertaining; indeed the description is as sorted best to the apprehension of those times, typicall and shadowie, but in such manner as never yet came to passe, nor never must literally, unlesse we mean to annihilat the Gospel.

The passage gathers together a number of Miltonic leitmotivs, most impressively working the concept of Reformation into the story of the "second temple" built after the return from Babylon—or at least, Reformation seems to hover over the interpretation of this part of the Old Testament history. The second temple, as Dryden reminds us in another, rather loaded context, "was not like the first." In fact it was not so splendid as its original and this entropic repetition must have been vaguely disturbing for Puritan readers of the Bible. Similarly, the Babylonian captivity is a dreary repetition of bondage in Egypt and difficult to interpret as in any way "progressive." Yet this is exactly what Milton proceeds to do, resorting to a typological reading in order to discern retrospectively a progress that can hardly have meant anything to the Jews themselves. Were their hearts at all "weaned from the Old Law" by the divine ordinance of the second temple? Rather, it is only in the dispensation of the Gospel that the weaning process can be detected, an origin of the sort where meaning catches up with memory. Once the typological significance of the second temple is established, however, the building of that temple in its own time must be distinguished from the fulfillment of the type set out in the text from Ezekiel. The type is reduced to figural status because it happens to be attached to a physical structure, and that structure is not what Milton really wants to talk about. Implicit also is the portending of this apocalypse in the success of the Reformation.

The argument in *The Reason of Church Government* charts a very complex movement of Milton's mind, a rapid arc from a point of origin in the past to a moment of apocalyptic annihilation; also from the "typical" origin to a time when those types must be taken "literally." Thus far I do not believe that I have said anything we do not already know about a certain kind of Reformation temperament. The next assertion is more polemical: from the stance of *Paradise Lost*, this concept of Reformation is a Satanic error. Here is Satan in a typological mood:

> O Earth, how like to Heav'n, if not preferred
> More justly, Seat worthier of Gods, as built
> With second thoughts, reforming what was old!
> For what God after better worse would build?
> (9.99–102)

Earlier in his career Satan has mistaken priority for the basis of an authority more absolute than God ordains, and he clings to this literal priority. The inversion of temporal valuations provides a very powerful defense against that earlier mistake by devaluing earliness itself as the "type" of what comes later. Satan would have "preferred" (put before) the second temple, and it devolves upon us to explain why God "after better worse would build." If this passage does indeed comment obliquely on a difficulty in the progressivist impulses of Reformation, the mysteriousness of the image in *The Reason of Church Government* is clarified. Satan is the agent of historical repetition masquerading as an advocate of progress. Eve is later persuaded, and Adam persuades himself, that she is "last and best" of God's creation. Milton perhaps mistook the second temple for this apocalyptic emblem when a truer image would be one of destruction, even the destruction of the temple. The "second temple," like Satan's "second thoughts," betrays the promise of Reformation to the binding down of historical repetition.

The first temple of the human spirit was Paradise itself, and the image of its destruction is to be found in book 11 of *Paradise Lost*, where its removal from Eden is given a pedagogic significance by Michael. In fact, the notion can be expanded now to comprise the thematic boundaries of the epic, which revises the concept of a third temple along apocalyptic lines; that is, the final temple, which the Book of Revelation identifies with the New Jerusalem, is not identical to the first but a thorough displacement into what looks like the category of the trope. We have been taught to regard this displacement ("thou dost prefer / Before all Temples th'upright heart and pure") as the thematic center of the poem, but it has not been sufficiently emphasized that the typological system producing this displacement is aberrant. Normal typology asserts only the correspondence between the type in the Old Testament and the antitype in the New. H. R. McCallum establishes the dominantly radical style of Milton's typology, which relegates all of the Bible to typological status. The antitype then is construed as either a present historical condition or a spiritual condition of the individual. The latter revisionary antitype seems to be figurative, but there is a curious wavering between the historical antitype (predictably, this as a literal event: apocalypse) and what might be called an apocalyptic state of mind. This shifting between significations of apocalypse corresponds to the distinction between the temple and the destruction of the temple as alternative typological emblems. Milton's stance as a prophet might be considered apocalyptic, a hypothesis evidently confirmed by recent studies uncovering the use of the Book of Revelation as a structural model for *Paradise Lost*. This textual repetition bears another interpretation, however, in the light of the larger historical failure within whose shadow the poem is written. There is, I believe, a conflict between apocalyptic and nonapocalyptic typologies enforcing a very un-Hebraic separation of history and prophecy. The conflict is inscribed in various subnarratives of *Paradise Lost*, one of which I will consider here, the story of Noah and the Flood.

Noah's story expands to fill a large part of book 11, and this fact is worth pondering because it so strangely unbalances the recounting of Old Testament history, overshadowing the more typologically significant covenant with Abraham. Milton is more interested in this narrative, certainly because it is the pretext for the destruction of Paradise, but even more for its apocalyptic resonance. Adam believes he has seen the end of the world, a mistake which logically extends the Satanic error in the Reformation mentality. But this is not to say that Milton is adopting the stance of historical disillusion; this would also be too reductive a "guess" at the heavy burden of the poet's intentions. I do not find that the angel Michael, if he is speaking for Milton, has entirely detached himself from his text of origin, John's *Apocalypse*, since he too eagerly moves on to the last days immediately upon concluding the story of Noah:

> but then he brings
> Over the Earth a Cloud, will therein set
> His triple-color'd Bow, whereon to look
> And call to mind his Cov'nant: Day and Night
> Seed-time and Harvest, Heat and hoary Frost
> Shall hold thir course, till fire purge all things new,
> Both Heav'n and Earth, wherein the just shall dwell.
>
> (11.895–901)

While this transition is warranted by Genesis, several other times in the course of his narrative, Michael suddenly overleaps whatever intervening historical time remains between the temporal present and the apocalyptic restoration of Paradise. Again, for example, at the story of Joshua:

> But Joshua whom the Gentiles Jesus call,
> His Name and Office bearing, who shall quell
> The adversary Serpent, and bring back
> Through the world's wilderness long wander'd man
> Safe to eternal Paradise of rest.
>
> (12.310–14)

And again at the return of Christ to Heaven:

> Then to the Heav'n of Heav'ns he shall ascend
> With victory, triumphing through the air
> Over his foes and thine; there shall surprise
> The Serpent, Prince of air, and drag in Chains
> Through all his Realm, and there confounded leave;
> Then enter into glory, and resume
> His Seat at God's right hand, exalted high
> Above all names in Heav'n; and thence shall come,
> When this world's dissolution shall be ripe,
> With glory and power to judge both quick and dead,
> To judge th'unfaithful dead, but to reward
> His faithful, and receive them into bliss,
> Whether in Heav'n or Earth, for then th' Earth
> Shall all be Paradise, far happier place
> Than this of *Eden*, and far happier days.
>
> (12.451–65)

Not until line 539 does the narrative catch up with Michael's proleptic urgency:

> till the day
> Appear of respiration to the just,
> And vengeance to the wicked, at return
> Of him so lately promis'd to thy aid,
> The Woman's seed, obscurely then foretold,
> Now ampler known thy Saviour and thy Lord,
> Last in the Clouds from Heav'n to be reveal'd
> In glory of the Father, to dissolve
> Satan with his perverted World, then raise
> From the conflagrant mass, purg'd and refin'd,
> New Heav'ns, new Earth, ages of endless date
> Founded in righteousness and peace and love,
> To bring forth fruits Joy and eternal Bliss.

These passages establish a rhythm of their own, quite discontinuous with the dismal repetitions constituting history. In fact Michael is rather reluctant to return to his primary narrative after his earlier apocalyptic flights, and he gives surprisingly short shrift to the New Testament "law of Faith" that seems so fundamentally involved with the progressive historical notions of Radical reformers. The two narrative postures exist in a state of tense disparity, but insofar as apocalypse is deferred, the rule of repetition prevails. Even the Story of Noah, with its thrilling prolepsis, is told twice (lines 712–62, and again at lines 787–839). The retelling is of course different, but this difference, as we shall see, is more an attempt to understand, than to deny the fact of repetition. Apocalypse cuts transversely across the primary narrative structure, without establishing itself within that rhythm. The accommodative moment in *Paradise Lost* locates itself somewhere in between, in an undefined space between repetition (history) and the event (apocalypse) which is always outside. It is the very sense of being halted, of not breaking through to an apocalypse, which builds up sufficient energy for the rhetorical release of sublimity. I think that English models of the sublime tend to emphasize this blockage (which is so conspicuous in Wordsworth) less for the peculiar turn taken by poetic theory in England than for the massive displacement of Miltonic energy from apocalyptic yearning for an end to history *into* the rhetoric of *Paradise Lost*. Later writers as a consequence receive Milton as the model of sublimity in English, even before there becomes generally available any theory, Longinian or otherwise, to analyze this model.

One other fact is illuminated by this recognition, the flattened tonality of the final two books of the epic, the occasion of so much registered disappointment. No longer should we identify the source of the problem with the reentry of history into the poem. On the contrary, history has up to this point saturated *Paradise Lost*, and in the final two books this matter has precipitated out. The sublime moment occurs not in the attenuations of historical chronology, but in rhetorical compressions that are charged with the premonitory rumblings of apocalypse: "He onward came, far off his coming shone." The condensation of temporality in such a line should be understood in this sense, gathering in one phrase a first coming, a *second* coming, and the feeling that this coming is both now and "far off."

If the possibility of sublimity is lost in the last two books of *Paradise Lost*, with their obsessive historical repetitions and equally obsessive proclamations of apocalypse, the analytical extension of the sublime moment is an invaluable aid for the interpreter. I would like to examine the historical paradigm as it disintegrates before our eyes, in the one place where that disintegration is most explicit: Michael's explication of typology in book 12. The passage is redolent with the self-inflating Puritan conviction of living in apocalyptic time, after the law has been abrogated:

So Law appears imperfect, and but giv'n
With purpose to resign them in full time
Up to a better Cov'nant, disciplin'd
From shadowy Types to Truth, from Flesh to Spirit,
From imposition of strict Laws to free
Acceptance of large Grace, from servile fear
To filial, works of Law to works of Faith.

This was the great guess about God's intentions, his historical "purpose," but history does not confirm this guess. What follows is another false apocalypse:

And therefore shall not Moses, though of God
Highly belov'd being but the Minister
Of Law, his people into Canaan lead;
But Joshua whom the Gentiles Jesus call,
His Name and Office bearing, who shall quell
The adversary Serpent, and bring back
Through the world's wilderness long wander'd man
Safe to eternal Paradise of rest.

(12.300–314)

It is as though Joshua *did* bring the Hebrews back to Paradise and not merely to Canaan. The typology works quite lucidly to indicate the significance of Joshua's name, but the grammar interrupts the historical rhythm with such a proleptic ambiguity that Michael must forcefully reinstate the repetitional narrative by the egregious reminder that the place of rest is to be distinguished from *earthly* Canaan: "Meanwhile they in thir earthly *Canaan* plac't."

Each of these moments of historical crisis fails to precipitate an apocalypse; even the death of Jesus, while it completes the *typology*, does not yet bring long wandered man to Paradise. The world proceeds from bad to worse. The structure that disintegrates here can be diagramatically expressed as follows:

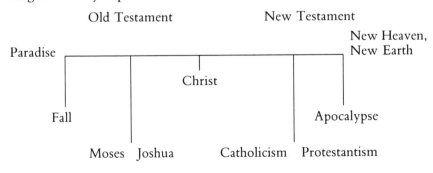

The typological sign, Moses-Joshua, even though it points to the antitype Jesus, corresponds *in context* to the transition from Catholicism to Protestantism, an antitype fully explicable after taking into account the accusations of regressive Hebraism leveled at the Catholic Church, as well as at backsliding Protestants. Types for Milton tend to locate themselves at such points of transition, which function much as the caesura at the center of a chiasmus. Indeed the entire structure is ideally a chiasmus, ABBA, but history seems lodged in the repetitions before the final reversal of BA. I have already associated the scheme of chiasmus with moments where the poet, or his epic characters, gather power to themselves after being stopped momentarily between the terms AB and BA. This hypothesis can be extended now to reconnect the end of this essay with its beginning. Chiasmus is the infrastructure of *Paradise Lost*, more important than any trope but functioning tropologically because the element of repetition is also a turn from an original signification. Schematically, a chiasmus "moves" or "turns" as follows:

A   B   B   A

Origin—Divergence—Repetition—Return

History can indefinitely extend the B term, innumerably multiply "second temples," but the basic pattern assures in some sense the inevitable return. Milton stands poised at one of these junctures, but the choice that presents itself is in the representation of the final A term: either a literal restoration of Paradise, or something different, a displacement into tropological language. Michael evidently chooses the latter ("paradise within") after some vacillation, a choice which lends particular interest to Milton's choice of *him*: the angel of John's *Apocalypse*. The reworking of the Book of Revelation is more thoroughly revisionary than Milton's current interpreters believe, especially as the structure of *Paradise Lost* is said to "imitate" the seven-part structure of John's book. "Paradise within" is a metaphoric displacement but it is also a transumptive allusion, revising its pre-text with a final structural echo of John's displacement of the temple into figuration: "And I saw no temple therein: for the Lord God Almighty and the Lamb are the temple of it." Milton goes just a little further: A visionary poet might have chosen to bring down the New Jerusalem; he does not.

    The two possibilities for construing chiasmus should finally elucidate the difficulty in Milton's representational language so vexing to readers like Dr. Johnson. The impulse to literalize is in a hidden sense apocalyptic, and Ithuriel's spear, as it touches off Satan's explosive return to "his own likeness" is a small rehearsal for the final conflagration out of which New Heaven and New Earth will arise; one assumes that Satan will be fixed thereafter in his true shape, eternally innocuous. Apocalypse comes in God's own time. When chiasmus is read in the time of "meanwhile" (and I interpret this temporality, of course, as the return of the *secular*), the restored Paradise becomes a trope for a state of mind as available to fallen Adam as to the society of Saints. We have only to distinguish now between this displacement and its Satanic parody, though I will always insist that these structures are more fundamental than any individual character's responses. Satan's parody of displacement ("the mind is its own place") precedes by the length of the epic Michael's turn to the "trope" of Paradise, but his reaction is no less a response to a failed revolution than Milton's poem is to its contemporaneous national failure. Satan's failed attempt to depose God cannot be so easily compensated by a turn to figuration. It makes a great difference that we have suffered through the turbulence of the epic, and even more that we have worked through a repetition of the apocalyptic text. The legitimacy of Michael's trope inheres not simply in its being a metaphor, but in its transumptive engagement with its biblical model, which engagement gives the metaphor a diachronic, historical meaning. The metaphor argues that the place does not matter, but the allusion asserts that the time does.

I would like the last words to be given to Christ, whose figure does not always satisfy but who most clearly struggles to embody the human rhythm of revisionary repetition. After the cold repetitions of the Father ("By some false guile pervert; and shall pervert"), and the unyielding antitheses ("Sufficient to have stood, though free to fall") the voice of the Son reestablishes the revisionary mode of chiasmus:

> O Father, gracious was that word which clos'd
> Thy sovran sentence, that Man should find grace;
> For which both Heav'n and Earth shall high extol
> Thy praises, with th'innumerable sound
> Of Hymns and sacred Songs, wherewith thy Throne
> Encompass'd shall resound thee ever blest.
> For should Man finally be lost, should Man
> Thy creature late so lov'd, thy youngest Son
> Fall circumvented thus by fraud, though join'd

> With his own folly? that be from thee far,
> That far be from thee, Father.
>
> (3.144–54)

Justus Lawler, in a recent study of schemata such as chiasm, argues that this scheme is "primarily representative of the intersection of the infinite and the finite," and if this metaphysics of rhetoric has any validity, it is here in the signature of Christ, the mark of the divine upon human history. Milton's Christ is always defined by the chiastic structure: he is "Love without end, and without measure Grace," a phrase that encloses the infinite (without end, measure) within the more accessible language of love and grace. The chiasmus, even in the form of Satanic parody, seems to embody for Milton that repetition which does not merely reflect the distance and terror of the Father's authority. We can only regret that the figure of Christ, the crossing of man and god, is not as great a poetic as he is a political success in the world of *Paradise Lost*. Critical conscience dissuades us from exalting him into the model of authority. That Milton struggles so hard to accommodate this figure, to find in him once again the resolution of history, suggests to me that authority is finally messianic, even the less urgent authority of literature. Poetic authority is difficult to understand just because it seems to "move" us without provoking that resistance we feel to the omnipresence of power. But *Paradise Lost* declares that literature is not exempt from these worldly vicissitudes, that it should move us even to resistance; and is this not another way of pointing to the poetic success of Satan? Milton's readers have either resisted him, or resisted with him. Inscribed in these versions of "filial freedom" is the conflict of literature and history, their false divorce and false reunion. If there were a sense in which we could "believe" in the messianic model, would that belief not signify the recovery of literature's idealized images for the world of history? Our agnosticism defers this apocalypse, but does not discover in the fact of duration an alternative to the sacred text. We remember that Shelley called time itself a redeemer, an even more inescapable Messiah.

"One First Matter All": Spirit as Energy

William Kerrigan

"Knowledge is as food": Poetry is as Digestion

During my analysis of Satanic self-creation I tried to summarize in Cartesian epigrams Milton's view of how human existence tends innately to unpack from itself religious existence: I think, therefore I am; I am, therefore I was created; I was created, therefore I am religious. I also suggested that the absence of a name for God, by introducing a need for metaphor and dislocating words from their given designation in a semantic search for God, establishes in unfallen language a poetics continuous with religious devotion. Returning to the nature of poetry from another angle, I would like to place a third Miltonic addendum beneath the *cogito*: I am religious, therefore I am poetic.

At the outset of his fine defense of Milton's style, Christopher Ricks concedes a few passages in *Paradise Lost* to his opponents, among them the "aridities" of angelic digestion. I sympathize to some degree. The Lucretian episodes we are interpreting seem at first glance arcane and dated, defended against ridicule by odd bits of discredited science, or simply boring in their distance from charged human event, like an "Aire and Angels" turned inside out in the manner of Benlowes or More, making love into a labored metaphor for pneumatology. But the second half of book 5 has special authority in *Paradise Lost*. It contains the axioms of reality. That this reality was carefully formulated, weighed in the poet's mind for two decades, everyone knows.

From *The Sacred Complex: On the Psychogenesis of* Paradise Lost. © 1983 by the President and Fellows of Harvard College. Harvard University Press, 1983.

But it is not widely appreciated that the success of the epic depends to a large extent on the kind of poetic effect that is the best defense of the ontological moments in book 5. This effect is offered, not imposed. If, however, we do not take the offer, the study of style will probably remain what it is in Ricks: the appreciation of local successes, the journey of the critical soul through bright fragments.

Paradise Lost is, after all, a poem of considerable length. In the memories of its nonprofessional readers such a poem may exist as an indefinite swirl. Who spoke second at the counsel of book 2? What happened during the second day of the civil war in heaven? When did Eve narrate her birth? Perhaps all has not been lost. Perhaps the reader has experienced some inarticulable improvement of sensibility. But one must insist that, if poetry survives by occasioning a revelatory redescription of the world, the poem as indefinite swirl is dead, a lost time, nor has the world been revealed. Of course the threat of this diffusion will be proportionate to the intricacy of the narrative, graver with respect to the *Faerie Queene* than with respect to *Paradise Lost*, and that is a point I mean to emphasize.

Milton's poem coheres for us, or has the possibility of becoming coherent for us, because he was able to root the entirety with logical and emotional force in certain privileged passages approximately as long as the bundles of "Ten, Twenty, or Thirty Verses at a time" in which it was composed. He was, as it were, able to assimilate the work of years to the work of some few visionary days, allowing his readers to treat themselves to an effect I call the "enfolded sublime." We know from the concept of the hermeneutic circle that interpretation involves the constant adjustment of part to whole and whole to part. But one trouble with fashionable talk about the hermeneutic circle is that this process shapes all experience and thus all reading, the cereal box you gaze at over breakfast and the late Heidegger that puts you to sleep: ubiquity invites reiteration. The enfolded sublime, on the other hand, is a high aesthetic achievement. It is the arrest of the hermeneutic circle, as if the poem were saying, "Stop here, I will occupy you." One problem with fashionable exhibitions of readers' responses is that the readers have not responded to this gesture, or else they would not read as they do, lost in the woods of endless self-correction and forever in quest of the poem denied them by their very procedure: process cannot yield solution. The enfolded sublime is not absolute closure. Yet by virtue of the enfolded sublime we have the poem, and having it, can proceed to ask our many questions.

The miniature of this effect is common enough in the doll's house of the lyric. During the seventeenth century poets such as Herrick and Lovelace made an aesthetic principle of "much in little," although it seems to me that these poets often give us much little and little much. In the long poem, however, the enfolded sublime is a rare effect available only from the greatest artists. Milton was its master. Spenser was not, as Milton told us:

> Not sedulous by Nature to indite
> Wars, hitherto the only Argument
> Heroic deem'd, chief maistry to dissect
> With long and tedious havoc fabl'd Knights
> In Battles feign'd; the better fortitude
> Of Patience and Heroic Martyrdom
> Unsung; or to describe Races and Games,
> Or tilting Furniture, emblazon'd Shields,
> Impreses quaint, Caparisons and Steeds;
> Bases and tinsel Trappings, gorgeous Knights
> At Joust and Tournament; then marshall'd Feast
> Serv'd up in Hall with Sewers, and Seneschals.
> (9.27–38)

Surely this should be added to what is reputedly the small number of humorous passages in the epic. It is perceptive humor. Commentators have noted only two of the three indictments of romance, leaving out the perceptively humorous one. This form glorifies the lesser heroism of war; its heroes and its battles are "feign'd" rather than historical. Yet Milton also indicts the genre for being "long and tedious," then condenses hundreds of poems and expanses of story into one catalogue of a day in the life of romance.

It is just this command of essence over detail that romance lacks—headless narratives stuffed with minute descriptions of the surfaces of objects. Although he assumed the obligation inherent in allegory of mastering with idea the proliferation of "tilting Furniture," Spenser was unable to arrest the spin of narrative in still points of enfolded sublimity. He tried to supply these well-wrought contractions, without which a long poem becomes long and tedious, destined to remain for most of its readers a complex impression rather than an event of meaning—Redcrosse surveying the world in book 1, Colin's interrupted vision in book 6, the bowers in between. But these moments, to make a long story short, are not able to ingest the bulk of the poem with sufficient elegance. Too much redounds. The hypertrophied and repetitious details in Spenser invite a labor of cross-referencing not unlike the order to be found in the Renaissance encyclopedia of synthetic knowledge. The poem, like the sense of the world that produced it, delays comprehension by multiplying allusion: "to understand this, see that," "to understand that, see this other." Meanings in literature are not of a piece; they have characteristic "shapes" or modes of presentation. The best student of Spenser, James Nohrnberg, accurately conveys [in *The Analogy of the* Faerie Queene] the meaning of the *Faerie Queene* as a texture of proliferating analogies no mind could survey at a glance. A single analogy is potentially infinite; we arrest the interaction when the two terms cease to reveal anything importantly new about each other. Lacking the enfolded sublime, which gives authoritative instructions to guide us through the maze of unfolding analogies, the parts of Spenser's poem weave themselves into each other with infinite stitches, and the only satisfactory alternative to a vague impression becomes the retention of the poem in complete detail—a work of art that, as a burden to memory, would have delighted the Ireneo Funes of Borges. But if Spenser is the Renaissance reproduced, Milton is the Renaissance understood.

The enfolded sublime is not available to a first glance. We realize this effect after the linear reading is finished, and even then it must be won by a reflection determined to have the poem, to make it occur as a thought. The moments selected can enfold no more than we are able to unfold. Since the entirety settles about these passages as if the poem had designated them its chosen reductions, they permit us a sense of provisional completion—an order subject to correction and elaboration, but of a higher level than the one we correct and elaborate in the linear process of reading: those who argue for the primacy of "interpretive decisions" in literary studies often transform a genuine philosophical issue into a specious *weltanschauung* by claiming that all such decisions are equally remote from external sanction; for it is not philosophy, but rather the trivial security of being irrefutable, to argue that every argument is decided by power or persuasion. Readers will differ, of course, over the ultimate sense of the poem arrayed about these moments, which drives everyone concerned back to the linear process of reading, and they will differ as well over the moments to be privileged. In fact, competing interpretations of *Paradise Lost* and other long works usually have their point of departure in a difference over the selection of the sublime passage. Practitioners of deconstruction typically enter the text at a moment traditional readings have thought insignificant, believing it to be subsumed in the controlling revelation of more famous passages, then labor to elevate this victim of oppression into a new sort of sublimity—I would be tempted to call it "unenfolded"—in which what is meant *and* what is repressed, or what cannot achieve direct expression so long as the meant is meant, are simultaneously focused. Since I am by no means opposed to this technique (what admirer of Freud could be?), I want to explain why I am endeavoring to merge psychoanalytic interpretation with an enjoyment, traditional in literary study, of the order enfolded in central passages. My first reason is simply that what is not meant in Milton is most eloquently not meant at crucial moments—when, for example, the Lady is left paralyzed after successfully repelling her tempter. Secondly, in the three late poems the psychological, philosophical, and theological "not meant" is in many ways, though not in every way, consistent with the manifest statement of the poem, and since this remarkable consistency seems to me the crux of Milton's achievement, I am trying to define it. Finally and obviously, the sublime coherence of these poems places us before the wisdom that can be acquired from the symbols of a major religion, many of which, the more so as Milton presented them, are held in common with another major religion.

Paradise Lost contains several examples of this effect. The poem coheres in different intonations about different centralities. While they prompt us to complete our sense of the entirety, the great enfolding moments offered to a reader of late Milton are perhaps unique in also representing a genesis: out of these passages the entirety, including, more or less explicitly, the poetic act, can be seen to have been derived. I have organized my discussion of the epic [in *The Sacred Complex*] about some of them. In the triptych of sublime visions at the transition from book 2 to book 3, Milton occupies the center, where he approaches the act originating everything in the act of creating his poem. I should explain that there is no contradiction between excellence in the enfolded sublime and my repeated stress on process in Milton, for I am speaking of the way in which the long poem presents its meaning or comes into coherence, whatever that meaning and that coherence be. At the center of the triptych is unmistakably a poet of temptation, conflict, and crisis: there he is, like a hyphen between antagonists, his poetic versions of Satan and God massed on either side of him, eyeing each other's works. Here the three dimensions of the sacred in the poem—the demonic, the human, and the divine—are contiguous, and Milton's deployment of the symbols found in these regions has a full epitome in the invocation to light. . . . In this [essay], seeking the acknowledgment of guilt required by the psychological balance of the invocation to light, I am tracing a spiral about the ontological speech beginning "O *Adam*, one almighty is." Already the promise of enfoldment has been heard. A sublime phrase introduces ontology—the "might" compressed between "al" and "is," the philosophical collision of "one" and "all," and the whole discourse prefaced by the gentle exclamation "O," which images visually the ideal circle of matter's return that the speech will proceed to explain scientifically and theologically. A few lines hence Raphael reshuffles these immensities in defining creation as unfolded from "one first matter all." One. First. Matter. All. These four words alone, fully heard, comprehend a great poem with much to say. To have them before us in a meaningful syntactic sequence is to be made momentarily giddy with the plasticity of huge meaning, able to present itself to us with harrowing abstraction, as when Satan at the end of book 2 enjoys a vision of our universe contracted into an atom of light ("O . . ."). The enfolded sublime seems to have been especially available, and especially sought for, at the end of the Renaissance. Descartes creates this effect, as do Kepler, Galileo, and Newton in their elegant reductions of copious motion to single formulae. On the pinnacle of *Paradise Regained*, in the double chorus on the triumph of Samson, and in a handful of masterful passages masterfully placed in the design of *Paradise Lost*, Milton was its poet.

I return to my widening gyre. Students of the Miltonic style cannot afford to discard the tabletalk of book 5, for there are clear indications that Milton intended to root poetry in the natural vitality of Eden; the "Holy rapture" of the "unmeditated" prayers at the beginning of book 5 (lines 147–49) has often been linked with the "unpremeditated Verse" (9.24) of the epic itself. We might be inclined to regard the element of spontaneity joining a digestive physiology and holy poetry as a casual association, despite a passage such as

> Then feed on thoughts, that voluntary move
> Harmonious numbers;

but book 5 has been designed to provide a logical development of this metaphor. Beginning as a medical ontologist, Raphael then becomes a "Divine / Historian" (8.6–7) in the epic mode, whose high matter will leave the ears of Adam "full of wonder" (7.70) and his intellect eager to "magnify" (7.97) the works of God. Understood systematically in the context of the axioms of reality, poetry continues at a higher echelon the refinements of the inner alchemist, making the relatively physical relatively spiritual. The possibility of this connection can be found in the ontological discourse itself. Thus "flow'rs and thir fruit" —terms for poetry and poetic invention familiar to Renaissance scholars, as for example in Sonnet 7 and the invocation or funeral lament in *Lycidas*—are "by gradual scale sublim'd" (lines 482–83). The next item in the first education of man awakens this sleeping significance. Poetry belongs to the movement of "all things" that "up to him return." In the passage cited [below] Milton [takes] note of his "strong propensity of nature" to inspire a nation and glorify the Lord.

> I began thus farre to assent both to them and divers of my friends here at home, and not lesse to an inward prompting which now grew daily upon me, that by labour and intent study (which I take to be my portion in this life) joyn'd with the strong propensity of nature, I might perhaps leave something so written to aftertimes, as they should not willingly let it die. These thoughts at once possest me, and these other. That if I were certain to write as men buy Leases, for three lives and downward, there ought no regard be sooner had, then to Gods glory by the honour and instruction of my country.

The art of such a poet—and Raphael is one—provides a channel in conscious life to express and refine the somatic appetite for wonder. Poetry is as digestion.

When Raphael, about to narrate the wars of heaven, defines the semantic strategy he has adopted to perform this task—presumably Milton's confession of his own strategy—he does not expect Adam to forget the previous lesson about nourishment. Comprehension of heaven, which Raphael gives to man, builds upon prior comprehension of the food which man gives to Raphael. Both activities strike an ontological relationship between "spiritual" and "corporal":

> yet for thy good
> This is dispens't, and what surmounts the reach
> Of human sense, I shall delineate so,
> By lik'ning spiritual to corporal forms,
> As may express them best, though what if Earth

> Be but the shadow of Heav'n, and things therein
> Each to other like more than on Earth is thought?
>
> (lines 570–76)

This much-debated passage on accommodated speech begins by likening the forthcoming epic, the first to be heard on earth, to the nourishment also "dispens't" for the "good" of man. At first it would appear
that much of heaven is an intellectual fruit beyond "the reach" of our
senses; if so, flimsy similes must be thrown across the void separating
two worlds distinct in essence. Then, through the example of objects
above having shadows below, "the reach / Of human sense" seems to
be capable of a true grasp, and the formerly earthbound similes delineate the actual relations between the two worlds. Madsen says that
"Milton is using 'shadow' here not in its Platonic or Neoplatonic sense
but in its familiar Christian sense of 'foreshadowing' or 'adumbration,'
and . . . the symbolism of *Paradise Lost* is typological rather than
Platonic." The epic teems with typology, but the shadow of these lines
has (with Miltonic adjustments) a Neoplatonic cast.

Insofar as Raphael addresses the dualists of Christian theology, his
questions about what "on Earth is thought" can only be audible to the
reader of the poem. But before we think of scholastic philosophers, we
must take account of the dramatic occasion: when has anyone "on
earth" ever "thought" his world excessively distinct from heaven? It
was just a moment ago, when Adam feared that the fruits of Eden
would be "unsavoury food perhaps" (line 401) for an angel. He was
told, as Raphael now reminds us, that human food "may compare
with Heaven" (line 432), and mistook truth for politeness:

> Inhabitant with God, now know I well
> Thy favor, in this honor done to Man,
> Under whose lowly roof thou hast voutsaf't
> To enter, and these earthly fruits to taste,
> Food not of Angels, yet accepted so,
> As that more willingly thou couldst not seem
> At Heav'n's high feasts to have fed: yet *what compare?*
>
> (lines 461–67; my italics)

The ontological discourse was the second and completer reply to this
incredulity. In context, Raphael's "though what if . . . more than on
Earth is thought?" is a professorial allusion to Adam's "yet what
compare?" and the answer he received. The angel's question is clearly

rhetorical, inviting Adam to reach for a truth he has already reached, since Raphael has just asserted that "things" in the two worlds come from "one first matter all" and are indeed "Each to other like, more than on Earth is thought."

The early pages of the *Christian Doctrine* propose an unusually positive theory of the truth-value of biblical metaphors for God. "Indeed he [God] has brought himself down to our level expressly to prevent our being carried beyond the reach of human comprehension." So guided, the exegete deduced from scripture his monist heresies. But if fallen education begins in the presence of the Bible, making hermeneutic procedures prior to ontology, Adam is educated in the order of things. He has an example from the world, an angel that really eats, to make the good sense of divine metaphor a logical deduction. Within the epic, then, monist ontology underwrites an unconventionally generous view of God's accommodation to man. As spiritual is to corporeal in the nature of things, so spiritual is to corporeal in the names of things: the universe being as it is, meanings borne on earthly terms can reach the lofty signification of heaven. Normally in Christian thought the fact that we can speak metaphorically of divine matters is a sign of our deficiency. God knows no metaphor. Here, however, words delineate: speech about heaven is not language in the act of defeating itself, straining hopelessly to capture the unnameable, but language realizing its potential to name everything. Raphael conveys these consequences of ontological monism through his two uses of the concept of likeness. "Lik'ning" refers to our usual notion of simile as a comparison with no stipulations outside its own framework, whereas "Each to other like" in his rhetorical question posits an ontological characteristic—similarity— inherent in the two elements of this linguistic similitude. Man and angel will not understand the same meaning, yet their different meanings will be "like" to the same extent that their different physiologies, rational powers, and worlds are "like"—"Differing but in degree, of kind the same" (line 490). Because Raphael can stoop to assimilate the food of Adam's world, Adam can rise to assimilate the meaning of Raphael's world. A heretical conception of the spirituality of matter issues in an unorthodox and optimistic conception of the materiality of spiritual discourse.

Seventeenth-century philosophers such as Ralph Cudworth were already attacking Hobbes and Descartes on the grounds that their efforts to speak of minds and things in a single vocabulary involved, in Ryle's phrase, a "category mistake," leading to anthropomorphism with respect to matter and misplaced concreteness with respect to mind. In using the word *res* to name both body and mind, Descartes alerted suspicious readers to the need to reexamine the foundations of the dualism he continually asserted. But it is important to recognize that Descartes committed the category mistake unwittingly: his intention was to distinguish between things in space and minds in time, not to confuse them. Milton, like Hobbes in this regard, committed the category mistake knowingly at the level of ontology; and if he also assumed—as he almost certainly did, it being an assumption so common in his times that it was hardly even noticed—that ontology would correspond to semantics in the event of truth, then there was to Milton's way of thinking no problem with category errors in language. Matter being the only category, the only "kind," those cases in which the vocabulary of things migrates into the description of mental life, and vice versa, evidence the power of language to mirror the world faithfully. Although his hope was to elevate matter rather than debase spirit, Milton proceeded with all the determination of a Hobbes to construct this all-purpose language, producing what we now call the Miltonic style. A graded continuum in the meanings of nourishment was his model case, and the meal of book 5 the foundation of his poetry, struck deep in reality.

Words and rhythms rooted in physiology at the material end of the monist continuum strive, like food itself, toward a higher state of application:

> But Knowledge is as food, and needs no less
> Her Temperance over Appetite, to know
> In measure what the mind may well contain,
> Oppresses else with Surfeit, and soon turns
> Wisdom to Folly, as Nourishment to Wind.
>
> (7.126–30)

When man and angel speak over their meal, they enact this trope, including its moral lesson. Once again Milton was aided in his semantic-ontological demonstration by the fact that many organizing structures in Renaissance medicine had arisen from projections of large and obvious processes, such as digestion, onto other activities of the organism, such as thought. In this passage, the "as" transforming healthy physiology into good knowledge is the signal of a scientific analogy, not a literary conceit. Renaissance neuroanatomists still accepted the general theory of the three cerebral cavities established by their medieval predecessors. The anterior cell of the brain, soft and moist, housed the *sensus communis* where the sensorium was formed from the input of the sensory organs and varied by imagination; the middle ventricle, warmest of the three, housed reason, which organized information passed back from the anterior cell into categories (the most general being similarity/dissimilarity), performing its acts of judgment; the third and final chamber, cool and dry, was the warehouse of information, the place of memory storage, admirably suited for retention by the firm case of the cerebellum. The underlying logic of this scheme is digestive, as Walter Pagel has maintained. What imagination gathered, reason separated and memory assimilated. The human brain collected, digested, and incorporated the material of the external world. Raphael is truly witty. "Knowledge is as food" is a proposition: unwanted data, the useless or the forgettable, was thought to escape in the form of vaporous spirits from the cranial sutures at the back of the head, and was actually called, in medical Latin, *flatus*. In the Renaissance the word "digest" meant "to order," as it sometimes does today. But what we now think of as the literal and abstract senses of the word had yet to be clearly differentiated even in scientific thought. Informed by metaphors understood as propositions, Renaissance medicine was an invaluable resource for someone presenting a monist universe in which concretion had to seem omnipresent.

The narrative of heavenly warfare is a good food offered to the "reach / Of human sense," its similes are to be understood on the basis of digestive similarities between heaven and earth, and the narrative itself shapes Satan's defeat in the "Intestine War" (6.259) as the evacuation from heaven of "what redounds": "but the evil soon / Driv'n back redounded as a flood on those / From whom it sprung, impossible to mix / With Blessedness" (7.56–59). The fates of food—eaten, assimilated or rejected—serve as the major "corporal" delineation in bringing all heaven before the sense of Adam. Satan turns wisdom to folly, and Milton captures his ironic contribution to his own defeat in a perfect and perfectly primitive accommodation. The rebel leader parodies Raphael's ontological speech in his hymn to the vitality of the underground, where things "dark and crude" strive for "ambient light" (6.472–83). Acting on his advice, the devils have "concocted and adusted" the "blackest grain" to charge their cannon. Its discharge condenses violent voidings—belching, vomiting, defecating:

> Immediate in a flame,
> But soon obscur'd with smoke, all Heav'n appear'd,

> From those deep-throated Engines belcht, whose roar
> Embowell'd with outrageous noise the Air,
> And all her entrails tore, disgorging foul
> Thir devilish glut.
>
> (6.584–89)

The volley has defeat written all over it. There is no more graphic and familiar instance of aggression against a nourisher coincident with aggression against the self than the rejection of food. On the third day a crystal wall "Roll'd inward, and a spacious Gap disclos'd / Into the wasteful Deep" (lines 861–62); while "Disburd'n'd Heav'n rejoiced," Christ drove the rebel angels headlong into this "mural breach" (lines 878–79). We have seen how food and appetite are extended to the temperate knowledge and wonder of the moral life in subsequent segments of Adam's education. In the end, as Raphael describes angelic copulation, nourishment is again the corporeality made spiritual. For when in human experience do we enjoy the object of our desire within us and mix totally? The sexuality of the angels conflates eating and pregnancy—a fusion already announced in the key word "fruit" (see Raphael's compliment to Eve and her meal at 5.388–91).

Begun concretely in the eating of a meal, and abstractly in the axioms of ontology, the progressive dilation of nourishment through books 5–8 instructs us in the ultimate good sense of a great complex of metaphors spread into every corner of *Paradise Lost*. One branch of this complex is Milton's variation on the old theme of the scatological devil; as indicated in the previous paragraph, nourishment takes our senses to hell as well as to heaven. Inversions and perversions of alchemical digestion, Michael Lieb has shown, characterize Satan throughout the poem. His negative alchemy turns sweetness into stench, vital life into the food of Death, all places into hell. His, too, is an alimentary universe, but one in which the purer feeds the grosser. Opposing him, the judgmental alchemy of God separates the saved from the damned, what can be assimilated and improved at the top of the universe from what must be evacuated and disowned at the bottom. After changing the fruit in the mouths of devils into ashes, God enunciates in digestive terms the irony of salvation history:

> I suffer them to enter and possess
> A place so heav'nly, and conniving seem
> To gratify my scornful Enemies,
> That laugh

. . . .
And know not that I call'd and drew them thither
My Hell-hounds, to lick up the draff and filth
Which man's polluting Sin with taint hath shed
On what was pure, still cramm'd and gorg'd, nigh burst
With suckt and glutted offal, at one sling
Of thy victorious Arm, well-pleasing Son,
Both *Sin,* and *Death,* and yawning *Grave* at last
Through *Chaos* hurl'd, obstruct the mouth of Hell
For ever, and seal up his ravenous Jaws.

(10.623–37)

In hell reside the unknowing housekeepers of God, busy with the chore of containing their own mess. The topos of the scatological devil is normally a simple strategy for heaping abuse on Satan, and it serves this function in Milton. But the resonances of digestion are so intricate and so orderly that this abusive rhetoric becomes embedded in a full portrait of Satan, and Satan embedded in a fuller portrait of the three dimensions of the sacred. As with "Knowledge is as food," the metaphor comes true.

Watkins in particular appreciated the poetic results of Milton's monism:

> We cannot overstress a fundamental truth about Milton which we find endlessly proliferated in his work. At his most creative, he accepts the whole range from the physical, specifically the senses, to the ultimate Divine as *absolutely unbroken.* This glad acceptance means that he is free to speak of any order of being (extending to inanimate matter) in identical sensuous terms as the great common denominator. . . . Few poets . . . have come so close to making what are ordinarily abstract concepts thus tangible.

Although Ricks does not cite Watkins, and makes nothing of monism, his observations time and again exemplify this statement. His remark about the "Tree / Of Prohibition" at 9.644–45 is typical of many of the local effects described in his book: "what begins as a moving and ancient metaphor (lead us not into temptation) crystallizes with terrifying literalness." These and other critics have taught us that Milton's ability to unite what Ricks nicely terms "incompatible greatnesses" appears with special clarity in his exploitation of the physical and moral senses of words such as *glory, amaze, oppression, height, place, supplant, end, wander, alienated, distance,* and *distaste.* He regularly gives us the impression that there is nothing alogical, nothing merely incidental about the polysemy of words: a good Miltonic word not only means in the realms of action and mentality, but meaningfully relates these realms.

Examples being many and familiar, I will limit myself to two. When Christ takes the field in the heavenly war, he commands the mountains to return to their bases:

> This saw his hapless Foes, but stood obdur'd.
>
> . . . .
>
> In heav'nly Spirits could such perverseness dwell?
> But to convince the proud what Signs avail,
> Or Wonders move th'obdurate to relent?
> They hard'n'd more.
>
> (6.785–91)

It is one thing to moralize about pride. It is monist poetry to offer the physical hardening of these "obdurate" wills, "gross by sinning grown" (line 661), as an ontological way of showing that it takes enormous concentration, not light carelessness, to deny the obvious. Milton halves the word "obdurate" and unfolds it as an idea of stubbornness and an occurrence—a prerational manifestation, a hardening landed before our senses. We are reading of the first situation that demanded the notion of "obdurate," and the poem recovers the birth of this idea in the *rightness* of a metaphor, as if hardening had been given to our senses in order that we might signify and understand pride. Milton incites us to think through the basis of an idea glossed over in moralizing talk about the "hardening of the will." The questions in the passage have exactly this effect: such pride is a mystery, not something well-understood. Freud was in fact anticipated by the poets, and much of what he said about the defense of denial, including the trope of defense, is available in contemplating this passage. Lastly, the first monist effect in the poem is the "fruit" dangling at the end of the opening line, both victual and consequence. The twinned epics of nature and moral action unfold from the torque of this word, which is varied constantly throughout the poem.

Monism also concerns the nature of the mimesis in *Paradise Lost*— what gets represented, what the poet cares about from episode to episode. As Watkins suggested, it provides a psychological encouragement before the fact, and a philosophical justification after the fact, for the wide childlike imagination of our poet. When approaching the transcendent, Milton does not set aside the categories of familiar experience; he insists on their application. The divine and demonic worlds are not concealed behind walls of paradox. Like a curious child, Milton is interested in how hidden things work (political counsels, the warfare and loving and marking of time in heaven, digestion), how things came about (imagine a catalogue of everything), and what things feel like (falling nine days, being hit by a mountain, having a rib extracted, changing into a serpent). Intellectual motives converging with psychological advantages in the creative process, he retained for his poetry strong vestiges of the tone and topography of our earliest researches into the world.

Milton resumed and renegotiated his Oedipus complex in the religious symbolism of his late poetry. The first complex remains in the poetry just as, in the best symbols, we often discern an implicit history, a prior experience "requesting" new meaning. The metaphor "time is a river," for example, propels us into a reflection about the riverness of time, but whatever we may gain from this reflection will be indebted to the phenomenal experience the metaphor both preserves and requests transcendence of—the small vertigo when the flow of the river, different and yet the same, presences the flow of time, different and yet the same. As time is a river, as God is the Father, Miltonic Christianity is the Oedipus complex. The principle guiding Milton's psychic life beyond the profane complex, whose settlement kept him a virgin for exactly half of his sixty-six years, to the sacred complex of his final poems, stands at the heart of his ontology in *Paradise Lost*. The entire poem is enfolded about it; the lower strives toward the higher, the earthly toward the heavenly, the unconscious sublimation toward poetic sublimation, without abandoning the concretion of the lower, earthly, and unconscious. The vitality of the body aspires and, in an unbroken continuum, passes over its task and its energy to the delineation of true wonders in religious poetry. This central nexus in the poem is an attempt to bring into awareness the creative process on the assumption that reason does not initiate the desire for meaning—once again, a Romantic theme emerging from Renaissance ideas. Developing his ontology poetically, Milton came closest to understanding the psychogenesis of his cultural achievement.

To prepare for the fall so loudly anticipated by the material of this chapter, I will present as clearly as I can a psychoanalytic view of this material. In the midst of this much emphasis on food there are surely archaic elements. The earliest sublimity of being at one with the mother, of recognizing on distinction between nourishment and nourisher, is discernible in Milton's conception of an inner alchemist that sublimates nourishment heavenward toward its nourisher, seeking to merge with "one first matter." This unconscious desire for the restitution of narcissistic love divulges itself in fantasies such as angelic copulation. Yet even here it is an oedipal ego—vulnerable in a solid body, subject to law, threatened with death for disobedience—before whom this fantasy is situated. Suffering in fact the fantastic tragedy of the oedipal child, Milton had been wounded, and his blindness was an epitome of many disappointments. Digestion had struck against his eyes. We have already noted [elsewhere] the narcissistic meaning of this event as the consequence of impure or poisoned nourishment from a weak-eyed mother and an embittered wife: stated bluntly in terms of the myth, Eve poisoned Adam. In his poem, although he made it Adam's first response, Milton rejected this narcissistic interpretation for an oedipal one. At the later and more "refined" level of the Oedipus complex, blindness was unconsciously construed as punishment, an interpretation supported by the many representations of intrusive and aggressive seeing in the poem. What of digestion at this stage of unconscious meaning? The phallus is the target of dismemberment because it is the organ of the sexual urge, yet the urgency of the Oedipus complex is more than sexual. Its phallus is the heir of a long attachment to the mother, and in this sense represents the earlier bond between child and mother: appetite loved her first; the penis symbolizes hunger. With the accuracy of justice, the father shot a dart at Milton's eyes from the organic system that loved, perhaps in all of us will always love, the early mother. Stated bluntly in terms of the myth, Adam fell because he could not sever himself from Eve.

But the lower aspires. When enmeshed in religious symbols, the Oedipus complex turns upon itself, submitting the ego to divine authority outside the traditions of men. In order to enter the sacred complex one must dethrone the profane superego by deriving a spiritual sonship immediately from God. Adam, to whom the philosophical, moral, and psychological education of books 5–8 is addressed, gives the imagination of the poet an entrance into this second oedipal alignment, since he is the only man besides Jesus whose father is God. The "universal blanc" of Milton's blindness requested new meaning and new authorization from the resources of his psyche. As we have stressed, once castration has been acknowledged in the first complex, obedience can also be motivated by the positive expectation of regaining in the future a semblance of the lost wish. This structure holds good, mutatis mutandis, in the second complex. How might Milton gain prophetic vision by identifying his blindness with the catastrophe of Adam? How might the logic of the sacred complex permit him to fulfill, in the name of justice, his poetic wish?

AN EXTRA SPIRIT, THE PATHOLOGY OF THE FALL, AND THE TWO CURES OF MICHAEL

The volcanoes of hell, the mining of Mammon, the dogs gnawing at the entrails of Sin, the dart of Death, the explosive belly of the cannon, the penetration of Eden, the poisonous dream poured into the ear of Eve, the possession of the serpent—throughout Milton associates Satan with violence to inner parts. The most lacerating of these assaults is of course the evil meal of book 9. But we cannot fully appreciate this violation without proceeding farther into Milton's physiological postulates. The friendly office of the inner alchemist, who guides our food across the boundary of traditional dualism, presupposes a substratum of organic matter stretched without break from dense body to rarified thought. To construct this ontological bridge from earth to heaven, a task parodied in the "Causey" (10.415) built by Sin and Death, Milton turned again to the speculations of hermetic Neoplatonists.

Galen's doctrine of the three bodily spirits was an incarnation in physiology of the Platonic soul. The liver produced "natural spirits" in the venous blood; the arterial chamber of the heart generated "vital spirits"; and the percolation of the blood through an intricate network of arteries, the so-called (and nonexistent) *rete mirabilis,* refined the "animal spirits" of the brain: life, passion, and thought were interludes in the upward journey of food through the bloodstream. Christian physicians inherited the problem of unifying this materialist hypothesis, developed in the matrix of Greek and Stoic pneumatology, with the doctrine of the immaterial soul. The usual solution was that the rational soul, being above the indignity of location, is entirely present in each part of the body; animal spirits circulating through the chambers of the brain function as but "the chariot of the soul." In Christian medicine, Galenic pneumatology survived by tightening man's double notion of himself, holding together a physiology (a theory of digestion) with a psychology (a theory of mental faculties modeled on digestion). Whenever orthodox theology or philosophy put the spirits in their place, the place was material. As Pierre Charron stated, "the Soule is in the bodie as the forme in the matter . . . and there is no mean or middle that doth unite and knit them together: for betwixt the matter and the forme, there is no middle, according to all Philosophie."

But when Donne spoke in a poem of the subtle knot of mind and body woven by these blood-begotten entities, he was closer to the spirit of spirits. Two analogies suggest themselves for the role of the spirits in Renaissance thought. The first is the appeal to *mana* in primitive mentality as defined by early anthropologists such as Durkheim, Mauss, and Lévy-Bruhl. *Mana* in their version of the primitive mind is an impersonal force suffused throughout the world that collects about powerful objects and powerful people. Its arrivals and withdrawals explain to men why things happen as they do—why that magic worked, why that man got sick, why that object is not to be touched by that other object. The spirits, similarly, were more than explanatory; they embodied the *principle* of causal explanation. Thus, when the chariot of God transports itself in *Paradise Lost*, this legerdemain does not merely happen, as something beyond the reach of explanation. It occurs as the effect of a cause, for the chariot is "Itself instinct with Spirit" (6.752). Spirits permeated Renaissance science, philosophy, theology, and poetry. Almost everything in the repertory of human behavior—sensations, acts of mind, love and lust, sickness and health, death—was open to causal definition by describing events in the invisible (you cannot check the evidence) but material (it is there nonetheless) paraworld of the spirits. The second analogy is with the "economic point of view" in Freud, which reduces mentality to the freeing, binding, and discharging of psychic energy. Accurate or not, Ricoeur contends, this energics made one of the vocabularies of psychoanalysis into a defensible "semantics of force" committed to representing desire *as* the pressure of a physical system [*Freud and Philosophy*]. Pneumatology equipped medieval and Renaissance man with his own rhetoric of force. When vital spirits cling to the image of a lady in the heart of a stricken lover or desert the heart of a quivering coward, we confront a reduction similar to Freud's cathectic energy. Motive becomes quantifiable, and as the immediate corollary of this reckoning, compulsive, a physiological tyranny to which lovers and cowards submit.

The explanatory power of pneumata received its grandest expansion in the work of Descartes. Spirits that could materialize the soul had another use: they could deanimate the body. In the medical spirits Descartes found a physical apparatus able to explain the vital motions of the body as an autonomous performance. Flesh was nothing but geometry in motion, spirits behaving spiritually, obedient to the laws of impact and hydraulic pressure. The horseman was out of the chariot. "Itself instinct with Spirit," the chariot had become a self-sufficient automaton not unlike those tricky creations sometimes placed in Renaissance gardens to move or sing by means of pressures fed through hidden pipes. We can detect a similar confidence in the scientific purity of pneumatic explanation in Bacon, Telesio, and other figures of the scientific Renaissance. Newton himself would look to them in search of a physical medium for the force of gravity.

In another tradition of Renaissance thought, mind was being fused with body, not subtracted from it. The God of the Neoplatonists, if pure idea, had spilled over into progressively more material emanations. Philosophers in this tradition, with their emotional interest in the ascent of contemplation and their intellectual interest in proving rationally the immortality of the soul, sought to define the precise gradations of mind's articulation with matter: earth and heaven might learn to communicate by means of substance. If infused with life, spirits that served in the soulless universe of Cartesian mechanism could serve with equal prominence in the vitalist universe of hermetic Neoplatonism. Agrippa and Ficino invoked the medical spirits to explain the ability of imagination to operate at a distance. In his *De triplica vita* (a title suggesting the Galenic tripartition of *spiritus*) Ficino argued that commerce between the magician and celestial inhabitants implied a kinship between astral matter and cerebral spirits. Pneumatology of this kind sanctioned an aggrandizement of the will; inspired by a Pelagian nostalgia for the astral powers given Adam in the *Corpus Hermeticum,* pious magi endeavored to reclaim the original dominion of man. By the time Ficino's magic reached Campanella, D. P. Walker has shown, similarity had become identity (*Spiritual and Demonic Magic from Ficino to Campanella*). Spirits, souls, and angels were consubstantial. *Spiritus* had come to supply the "middle term" denied by orthodoxy, and all traffic between earth and heaven could be rerouted accordingly.

Alexander Ross, the furious watchdog of convention in seventeenth-century England, acknowledged that ordinary language invited such excesses. Although the single word "spirit" denoted bodily substances, souls, and angels, souls were not medical spirits, and neither souls nor medical spirits were angelic. Weemse also cautioned against accepting the false lure of polysemy. But Milton saw truth liberated where the dualists saw language abused:

> one first matter all,
> Indu'd with various forms, various degrees
> Of substance, and in things that live, of life;
> But more refin'd, more spiritous, and pure,
> As nearer to him plac't or nearer tending
> Each in thir several active Spheres assign'd,
> Till body up to spirit work, in bounds
> Proportion'd to each kind. So from the root
> Springs lighter the green stalk, from thence the leaves
> More aery, last the bright consummate flow'r
> Spirits odorous breathes: flow'rs and thir fruit
> Man's nourishment, by gradual scale sublim'd
> To vital spirits aspire, to animal,
> To intellectual, give both life and sense,
> Fancy and understanding, whence the Soul
> Reason receives, and reason is her being,
> Discursive, or Intuitive; discourse
> Is oftest yours, the latter most is ours,
> Differing but in degree, of kind the same.
>
> (5.472–90)

Everything is in transition. The root metamorphoses into stalk, stalk into leaves, and leaves into flower, whereupon the plant offers its being to man, "bright" only to one who sees and "odorous" only to one who smells. The bright essence at the summit of vegetable aspiration then becomes the root of human aspiration. If we assume that in the phrase "Man's nourishment" the "flow'rs and thir fruit" have already been refined to natural spirits, there are again four stages in the human sublimation: natural spirits (root), vital spirits (stalk), animal spirits (leaves), and intellectual spirits (consummate flower). Like the "bright" and "odorous" flower, the consummate refinement of man lifts his "being" into communication with a higher order of creation, the "kind" of heaven. The extended meanings of "spirit," far from treacherous, correspond to ontological process. Milton has ventured the radical equation of cerebral spirits, souls, and angels.

A modification in Galenic pneumatology accompanies this equation. To the three bodily spirits Milton has added a fourth or "intellectual" spirit, complementing the familiar distinction between discursive and intuitive reason with a heretical physiological distinction. As Babb explains, the poet "assumed—or deduced—the existence of a material intellectual spirit which is the substance of the angels and which man alone among earthly creatures possesses, and thus he bridges the gap between man and angel." Because reason is divided into discursive and intuitive and man produces animal and intellectual spirits "whence the Soul / Reason receives," the natural inference would be that animal spirits operate in the lower sort of knowing, which is temporal and logical, while intellectual spirits operate in the higher sort of knowing, which is simultaneous and nondeliberative. Had man remained obedient, he would have become "all spirit" like the angels—predominantly intellectual spirit, angels being "pure / Intelligential substances" (5.407–8). The unfallen life of man contains numerous instances of intuition's cooperation with "discourse." It is the power by which Adam knows God before finding him ("Whom thou sought'st I am"), dreams realities, and gives voice to the created order in "Unmeditated" prayers. Considered physiologically, which is one of the ways Milton chose to consider it, the fall is a disaster for the intellectual spirit especially.

Satan twice attacks the spirits of man. With the "devilish art" of book 4, he tries to "taint" the "animal spirits" of Eve by his dream of false ascent (lines 804–5). But "Evil into the mind of God or Man / May come or go, so unapprov'd, and leave / No spot or blame behind" (5.117–19). To think through an evil action in the discursive mode, whether awake or dreaming, is blameless. A taste that puts an end to thought precipitates the fall. At that moment evil reaches inward to bring "spot" and "blame," a guilt inseparable from physical stain, to all the spirits. Representations of digestive illness surround the crisis. At each disobedience nature suffers the cramps of a bellyache, "Sighing through all her Works" (line 783) and trembling "from her entrails" (line 1000). These macrocosmic symptoms in the body of mother earth herald the arrival of a pathogenic nature, corrupt with flatulence: "Vapor, and Mist, and Exhalation hot, / Corrupt and Pestilent" (10.694–95). But an endogenous source of disease is born simultaneously in the inner weather of man's storm-tossed pneumata. The "dilated Spirits" (9.876) praised by Eve have actually become "Encumber'd" (9.1051).

Unfallen love sponsored the refinements of digestion. As the inner alchemist sublimates nourishment "by gradual scale" until "body up to spirit work," so true love "refines / The thoughts" and "is the scale / By which to heav'nly Love thou may'st ascend" (8.589–92). The first "operation" attributed to the fruit is the reorientation earthwards of love's alchemy:

> but that false Fruit
> Far other operation first display'd,
> Carnal desire inflaming.
>
> (9.1011–13)

These are the fires in which you burn, akin to hell as the heats of unfallen digestion were akin to heavenly vitality. "There they thir fill of Love and Love's disport / Took largely" (line 1042–43). Lust, too, is an intemperate meal. Our disobedient parents move as the chariot wills, subjected to a physiological "operation."

The Pelagian program of Renaissance hermeticism has now been banished to the far side of human evil. "No more" will men enjoy the "Venial discourse" with angels (9.1–5) that occult philosophers hoped to promote through pneumatology. Spirits as vehicles of aspiration, leading the will intuitively toward God and the flesh naturally toward an intellectual body, belong to our prelapsarian condition. The intimate defilement of the fruit founds a new psychology on a new biology:

> Soon as the force of that fallacious Fruit,
> That with exhilarating vapor bland
> About thir spirits had play'd, and inmost powers
> Made err, was now exhal'd, and grosser sleep
> Bred of unkindly fumes, with conscious dreams
> Encumber'd, now had left them, up they rose
> As from unrest, and each the other viewing,
> Soon found thir Eyes how op'n'd, and thir minds
> How dark'n'd.
>
> (9.1046–54)

A "force" has violated "thir spirits" even to the "inmost powers." The meal that Satan promises will transform mankind into angels does transform us—but into the opposite of angelic freedom. "Necessity and Chance," God proclaims, his words appropriate in kind if not in degree to angels, "Approach not me, and what I will is Fate" (7.173–74). At the fall, necessity invades man and his will must expend great energies on adjusting to fate rather than creating it. With the "mortal taste" of that fallacious fruit, pneumatology becomes for the first time in Eden a semantics of reduced volition, a vocabulary that tells of an "operation" that "Made err," conveying the surrender of mankind to appetites in excess of biological need. If intuition is the transcendence of will in apodictic knowledge, intemperance is the debasement of will in mechanistic desire. From this one choice, choice will forever be conditioned by "dark'n'd" impulse, by illusion and by bitter conflict. This new order of mechanistic intemperance, Michael informs Adam, will cause "Diseases dire" (11.474). Satan has managed to fray the bright thread joining immortal man to immortal angel:

> As with new Wine intoxicated both
> They swim in mirth, and fancy that they feel
> Divinity within them breeding wings
> Wherewith to scorn the Earth: but that false Fruit
> Far other operation first display'd.
>
> (9.1008–12)

In this brilliant passage we behold the unfallen destiny of man transformed into an illusion of inebriation, the false promise of a mere wish, and worse than that, a defensive wish, for all the while an "operation" weighs them downward in wingless obedience to gravity to copulate on the ground.

One consequence of impaired intuition, the "inmost" of human "powers," is damage to the "self-knowing" constitutive of man:

> Thus they in mutual accusation spent
> The fruitless hours, but neither self-condemning,
> And of thir vain contest appear'd no end.
>
> (9.1187–89)

Milton ends the book of the fall with the insight that judgment, turned away from the recognition of inmost crimes, will tend hereafter to operate more accurately with respect to the other than with respect to the self. Subsequent lapses in intuitive apprehension measure how darkened their minds have become, as Adam and Eve reason inconclusively about the nature of death and think to abort posterity through sexual abstinence or suicide—the desire to die, which will also be expressed in the "Lazar-house" of book 11, where diseased humanity begs relief from a perversely tardy Death (lines 491–93), being the definitive slavery of the mind to the sovereign imposition of a fallen body in a fallen nature.

Intuition survives in their hopeful suspicions about the "mysterious terms" of divine judgment. But, leaving aside the rare miracle of assumption whose interest for Milton I have treated elsewhere, the pathogenesis of the fall is irreversible. Adam receives from Michael a full exposition of the new rhetoric of force. As the reader had been led to expect, the natural death in the future of fallen Adam is a perfect inversion of the natural elevation in the future of unfallen Adam, as if the first physiology had been turned over and dropped, producing a headlong fall toward brute matter: "in thy blood will reign / A melancholy damp of cold and dry / To weigh thy Spirits down, and last consume / The Balm of Life" (lines 534-46). Lifeblood itself is subjected to a weight. Whereas Raphael enticed Adam with a physiology of aspiration, body working up to spirit, Michael sobers him with the physiology of fatality, spirit working down to body, that will in time become the object of medical science. The body is now, as it has never been before, the dominion of necessity over wish. Under the reign of leaden melancholy, the downward course of the spirits duplicates as mere process the downward plunge of desire into mechanism observed at the fall. Death is the biological repetition compulsion of our primal crime. Like Satan, we "consume" ourselves in the end.

For centuries Christian theologians had rigorously dissociated the forbidden fruit from the magical potions consumed in Homer and Ovid. Milton adopted this tradition in his treatise on doctrine. Inherently the fruit was no more than a fruit: "It was called the tree of knowledge of good and evil because of what happened afterwards: for since it was tasted, not only do we know evil, but also we do not even know good except through evil." But in the epic real symptoms—intoxication, digestive vapors, restless sleep, darkening mind—are predicated of the fruit. At the very moment it is first tasted, Milton is oddly uncertain over its inherent quality: "such delight till then, as seem'd, / In Fruit she never tasted, whether true / Or fancied so" (lines 787–89). Why is he unwilling to say whether the forbidden fruit is really the sweetest one? Sweetest or not, he has given us the material to build a fairly strong case for its having been poison fruit. Because the sentence of death is being carried out by "The Law I gave to Nature" (2.49), Milton might have decided that it would be efficient and forward-looking of God to have put death in the fruit—in which case "fallacious" Satan lied to man about the *particular* "force" of the fruit and not about its forcefulness. Favoring this view would be Milton's reluctance elsewhere in his monist poem to separate the letter from the spirit of his metaphors. The question cannot be decided absolutely, and in any case nothing much hangs on its outcome:

however God executes the sentence, man ate and man dies. The fact that there *is* a question tells us more than its answer would. Milton has made the pathogenic fruit in his Lucretian narrative of the fall concrete enough to belie easy translation into mere metaphor. Before us, in a primary way, are the signs of an illness.

It comes as no surprise that Adam requires the attentions of a physician. The angel ministers to his need:

> but to nobler sights
> *Michael* from *Adam's* eyes the Film remov'd
> Which that false Fruit that promis'd clearer sight
> Had bred; then purg'd with Euphrasy and Rue
> The visual Nerve, for he had much to see;
> And from the Well of Life three drops instill'd.
> So deep the power of these Ingredients pierc'd,
> Ev'n to the inmost seat of mental sight,
> That *Adam* now enforc't to close his eyes,
> Sunk down and all his Spirits became intranst:
> But him the gentle Angel by the hand
> Soon rais'd, and his attention thus recall'd.
> *Adam,* now ope thine eyes.
>
> (11.411–23)

Michael removes two obstructions from the head of Adam. There is nothing metaphorical in the presentation of the first cure; the passage opens with the founding of our medical tradition. Like the physicians known to Milton, the angel can lift an incipient tumor and purge the optic nerve with "Euphrasy and Rue," curative herbs used commonly during the Renaissance for disorders of the eye. Fruit as victual "Had bred" fruit as consequence, depositing a film in the eyes of man: in the materialistic narrative coincident with the moral narrative, Adam was developing cataractic blindness from the unpurged vapors of the fruit. Then Michael clears a pathway to "the inmost seat of mental sight." His cure of this second obstruction does indeed leave empirical medicine behind. The angel administers three drops "from the Well of Life"—a wishing well nowhere mentioned in the rest of the poem. By the end of the passage Milton has at last severed medicine from miracle. Here certainly is a "wonder."

But the affliction treated in the second cure is no less physical than the film bred in Adam's eyes. Recalling the "inmost powers" invaded by the force of the fruit, the "inmost seat of mental sight" must be the habitation of the intellectual spirits. Michael renovates that intuitive power manifest in visionary dreams and unmeditated songs. Adam is now being readied for another education, and enabled to see, in the temporary brilliance of his forthcoming visions, what Michael intends him to see. Reestablishing the frayed link between man and angel, prophecy considered as a physiological event demands a new enlightenment of the intellectual spirits. Immediately "all his Spirits" fall into a holy trance, prepared to be taught the new ways of God.

Milton implies that, beyond death and disease, the material price of the fall was to make the innermost treasure of the spirits of intuition virtually inaccessible by natural means. If we carry a paradise within us, we carry also a paradise lost within us. This fruit of original sin will never be the province of medical science, for nature operating naturally in the body pulls intuition down to deliberation in the inevitable descent of the oppressed spirits. Such a recovery can only be "enforc't" from above by the radically exogenous cure of inspiration: as a countermeasure to the "force" invading our darkened minds at the fall, the three drops touch the spotted parts of the mind as intimately as the fatal fruit. Divine intervention of this kind will be known throughout human history in the Protestant guidance of the "spirit" within. It is felt by an "enforc't" Samson when he suddenly loses his will and gains divine purpose, declaring, "I begin to feel / Some rousing motions in me" (lines 1381–82). In *Paradise Lost* Milton represents the first of these benign intrusions by the (for once) Trinitarian dosage from the "Well of Life." What can the Well of Life be, given the suppositions of the epic, but the pure vitality of God that has, through the fateful act of creation, merged indissolubly with "one first matter"? Inspiration is a second gift of life for man.

It will take our argument back to the psychological drama of the creative process to note the serious theological repercussions of presenting the fall as a pathogenic event reversing the upward aspiration of *Paradise Lost*'s ontology. Milton held in the *Christian Doctrine* that the fruit was forbidden for no other purpose than to manifest our obedience: "it was necessary that one thing at least should be either forbidden or commanded, and above all something which was in itself neither good nor evil." But the forbidden fruit of the epic cannot be, as many critics have alleged, the orthodox "arbitrary fiat" defended in the treatise. Perhaps no coherent poem could preserve this doctrine unless it were the author's overwhelming intention to do so, since good art tends by nature to make its details seem inevitable. However that may be, the God of this poem could not have prohibited any other action, such as standing on one's head, slapping a face, or spitting into the wind, without changing altogether the meaning of the fall. Eating embodies ontological and historical rhythms; the semantic dilation of food to knowledge, appetite to wonder, and temperance to obedience can be traced in much more detail than I have attempted. The fall focuses a great design of unbroken harmony. Seeking forbidden nourishment is not, as given sense by this design, a crime solely because of arbitrary authority: it is *the* trial and *the* crime, the ontologically appropriate crime, its wrongness shot through the texture of Milton's universe. The forbidding is not arbitrary: it is "necessary," as the treatise grants, in order that there be obedience and therefore virtue. That this one fruit was forbidden may well be arbitrary, although its effects would not appear to be those of just any fruit, and Milton himself allows that it might have been the tastiest one. In its ultimate good sense this poem *attacks* the severe voluntarism that some critics believe Milton to have espoused. Milton directs this attack, furthermore, at voluntarism's seemingly impregnable instance: "But of the tree of the knowledge of good and evil, thou shalt not eat of it: for in the day that thou eatest thereof thou shalt surely die" (Gen. 2:17). Huge blocks of prehistory context this law in *Paradise Lost*. The more we learn about Milton's universe, the more we learn that we are "of kind" to be able to know more, and the more we suspect that, if we did, God might be justified apart from any deep concern with his absolute will. Is Milton resisting the God of incomprehensible power in the sacred complex, evading a feared encounter with sheer will? Is he lessening the otherness of the law, which would be a step toward assimilating the superego into the ego?

To an extent, undeniably. Absolute voluntarism, a divine will of power alone, is the theological position given to Satan in the poem. God is not always so riddling and involuted as he was with Samson, and sometimes the inner oracle of *Paradise Regained* will sanction a rational doctrine "granted true." When imagining the institution of the first law, Milton tried to mitigate Satan's view of a fearfully irrational God. (That sort of deity would appear soon enough in the tale of Abraham and Isaac, which Milton interestingly omitted from his selective Bible in books 11 and 12.) In any event, the monist ontology of the epic does not imply that Milton would have preferred reason to be a law unto itself, rendering divine commandment superfluous. Ontological appropriateness is a long way from the suggestion that reason might have *discovered* the law, which is the only real opponent of voluntarism in Christian theology, and a rare one at that—Aquinas on the Decalogue, Kant on the categorical imperative, a few lesser figures in the history of Christian ethics. Understood within the entirety of *Paradise Lost,* the law against eating a particular food is not so much generated by reason as it is a revelation to reason. Our sense of its appropriateness arises from what the poem has taught us about those elements of our humanity that lie beneath reason, disturbing its false autonomy—the biology and psychology of man, creature of complex appetites. There can be little doubt that Milton felt his way to this appropriateness, not in the empyrean of pure reason, but in the experience of *gutta serena.* Blindness as interpreted by seventeenth-century medicine supplied him with the history of what transpired in the secret recesses of the body when man ate "the Fruit / Of that Forbidden Tree, whose mortal taste / Brought Death into the World, and all our woe."

Andrew Marvell was a reader of acute intuitions.

> the Argument
> Held me a while misdoubting his Intent,
> That he would ruin (for I saw him strong)
> The sacred Truths to Fable and old Song
> (So Sampson grop'd the Temple's Posts in spite)
> The World o'erwhelming to revenge his sight.

Marvell feared, "while misdoubting his Intent," that Milton would collapse the temple of "sacred Truths" into the ruins of "Fable and old Song," revenging himself on the God he ostensibly came forth to justify. In fact, the purgative denial of this very aggression is writ large in the poem Milton solicited from his God. He destroyed the unfallen world with "Death" and "all our woe" in the act of accusing, not the theft of his sight, but the fate of his blindness. In the etiology of his condition, nourishment had turned to wind, a gross vapor had solidified in his optic nerves, obstructing his spirits and darkening his eyes. Blindness to Samson is "a living death": "Myself my Sepulcher, a moving Grave, / Buried" (lines 100-103). Although Milton never expressed this agony in his own voice, he must on occasion have seen death in his blackness, such as the "murmur" recorded in Sonnet 19, where his "dark world and wide" is a living anticipation of the "death" of the unprofitable servant in the parable of the talents, cast into the "outer darkness" (Matt. 25:30). As he wrote his epic in Genesis, this blindness by digestive failure became the sin tainting all men, a hardened infection whose cause, like the tumors in his eyes, could not be expunged. The taint Adam suffered has been fixed in our solid flesh: through our first Parents, we have all supped full of horrors. The reversal of ontological aspiration, condemning the body to weight and fixity, makes *gutta serena* the radical instance of an illness everywhere to be found·in fallen biology and fallen psychology. Milton recorded his own ongoing struggle with the general pathology in the last words of his last invocation:

> unless an age too late, or cold
> Climate, or Years damp my intended wing
> Deprest; and much they may, if all be mine,
> Not Hers who brings it nightly to my Ear.
>
> (9.44–47)

Continuing the tradition begun with Michael's renewal of "the inmost seat of mental sight," the flight of inspiration must contend in a fallen mind with melancholy "damp" and "deprest" spirits. These forces may be held in abeyance for a time, but there is no escape, as there was in *Comus,* from growing "clotted by contagion." The epic poet has already been struck by our virulent common illness. It is not to be dispensed with. On the contrary, his effort is to secure from this weakness, fully acknowledged as weakness, his creative power.

He never solicits the double cure given unimplored to Adam. The theme of the Lucretian epic in *Paradise Lost* pursues in another register the theme of "better fortitude" governing its epic of heroic action— our restricted freedom and our acceptance, without indicting God, of a world no longer to our wish. To be the proponent of this theme, the poet must be a true poem, containing "in himselfe the experience and the practice of all that which is praiseworthy." The physiological representation of the fall, ending with Adam being cured from incipient cataracts, demonstrates the fit between the life of the poet and his art. More importantly it reveals that Milton has mastered the moral valor he celebrates. To Adam is given the happy cure Milton no longer expects. He will not bargain with God over his blindness, nor will he defend himself against his loss, as he did in the Second Defense, by idealizing the deprivation. The poet deals *with* his blindness.

"So much the rather thou Celestial Light / Shine inward." We left the invocation to light with the conviction that its reversal of the formula of debt, making God the obligatee and Milton the obligator, would not be psychologically coherent unless blindness were a punishment owed for the potential trespass of the poem he had yet to write. And that is precisely what it is. "Blindness must not be considered a judicial punishment." Not a judicial punishment, the sentence specific to a given crime, but a punishment, a sign in his flesh of the communal guilt of original sin, and the means by which Milton could identify himself with Adam, for whom the physiological deterioration making him vulnerable to blindness *was* a judicial punishment. The poem indicts blindness as a fate justly deserved. To justify the ways of God in a personal sphere was to conceive of his condition as unalterable, as punishment, and still as just. Completing this private theodicy in his representation of "Man's First Disobedience," Milton links blindness to the primal crime of Adam, thus indicting himself rather than God, and as the flesh of Adam assumes responsibility for the sentence of *gutta serena*. He can therefore fulfill in the name of justice his desire to see "what surmounts the reach / Of human sense." He has suffered the punishment due for whatever may be unlawful in such ambition, and suffered it *as lawful*, the just imposition of a just God. Having created the wish to be invulnerable in the flesh, indulged the desirability of this wish, and then, without indicting God, sacrificed this wish, Milton can rightfully claim his due: "to see" (as Adam and Michael see in book 11) "and tell" (as Adam and Michael tell in book 12) "Of things invisible to mortal sight." *As blindness is equivalent to the curse of the fall, so the writing of the poem, which the guilt of this blindness paid for, must be unconsciously equivalent to the guilty aspiration of the fall.* It was because of its intrusive curiosity that this literary project was "long choosing, and beginning late," and it is evident in the poem that Milton's appetite for wonder exceeds on "bolder wing" the limits set for Adam.

The feeling that one has been punished before one has become worthy of a guilt that would motivate and the punishment is intrinsic to our lives. If it were not, no one would bother to ask the murmuring questions that lead to a theodicy. From the beginning, long before we are able to discern power from justice, we have been sentenced to disease and death. The Romantic criminal, sensing the arbitrary exaction of these penalties, feels free to disregard justice altogether. But Milton defended the justice of our condition, while in the same breath satisfying his desire to violate mortal limits. Unlike the Romantic criminal, whose archetype in our literature is his own portrait of Satan, he was able to avail himself of the redemptive paradoxes of Christianity: to fall is to rise, to be guilty of unfettered desire is the way to attain unfettered desire. If the writing of the poem is unconsciously equivalent to the guilty aspiration of the fall, that aspiration is ironically equivalent, in the manifest meaning of the poem, to the future outlined for unfallen man. The doubling of unfallen and fallen aspiration permits a moral sublimation in the psychology of the aspiring poet. We can infer the achievement of this sublimation from the paradoxes inherent in the formula of the transposed debt. The potentially guilty act of writing the poem is justly owed to Milton, provided that he indict his blindness as a morally just punishment: the potentially guilty act is therefore morally just, for as the poem must be written, Milton will justify the ways of God to all men, including himself.

The same redeeming sublimation can be inferred from the imagery of blindness and sight. *As blindness is punishment, so seeing is forgiveness, and the visionary composition of the epic renders the poet symbolically guiltless.*

> What in me is dark
> Illumine, what is low raise and support;
> That to the highth of this great Argument
> I may assert Eternal Providence,
> And justify the ways of God to men.

The "great Argument" of a private theodicy, requiring Milton to condemn his blindness as the summation of what is "dark" and "low" in mankind, is the psychological plot of the poem's creation, the means by which "I may assert" became "I did assert." At the center we have circled about in discussing the wish evoked in books 5–8 and its disillusionment in book 9: in order to claim prophetic vision, and become in that sense guiltless and unfallen, Milton must purge through moral accusation another version of the same wish, demonstrating that his desire not to be blind, guilty, and fallen contradicts the justice of God. This, rather than the defensive stainlessness projected in *Comus,* is the happiest strategy of the oedipal child. To achieve the wish, first slay the wish. Elevating the complex to religion, Milton restaged its sad yet heroic drama of relinquishment, achieving its resolution in a work of art that spent with passion his hoarded talent.

Prophecy for the late Milton was a partial and exceptional relief from the pressures of the fall. For the few and by the few, prophetic missions could not serve the grand hopes of utopian Christianity or the quasi-scientific visions of reconquering through pious magic the dominion of old Adam. But these currents of Renaissance ambition touch his work nonetheless. Milton believed himself to have undergone a privileged recovery from the second disease cured by Michael. His mind irradiated "through all her powers," he repossessed the intellectual spirits darkened and dissipated by the trauma of our first crime—lodged in us useless—to enjoy once again the watch of inward sight with its gifts of unpremeditated song and true prophetic vision. His renewal of the intuitive powers originally implanted "inmost" in man trails with it the Pelagian aspirations checked at the fall. Heaven is again in communication with earth. Again a man is reasoning with the unpremeditated grace, the poise of voluntary and involuntary, characteristic of intuition. His eyes how darkened, but his mind how opened!

The metaphor deep-rooted in *Paradise Lost* for the poem itself is the angel body. Composing book 3, its poet has actually visited heaven and "drawn Empyreal Air, / Thy temp'ring" (7.14–15), reclaiming in art the lost destiny of the human body. With the "sense variously drawn out from one Verse into another," its unobstructed lines forsake the "vexation, hindrance, and constraint" of rhyme, stanzaic pattern, gnomic syntax, and other restrained conveyances in the corpus of poetry. Elevating deliberation to the higher state of intuition, its unpremeditated flow joins earth and heaven. It will allow no dismemberment in the nature of things, for that would leave a blind poet as "Cut off" from the ways of God as he is from "the cheerful ways of men." Resting on a substratum of "one first matter," it boasts a language able to name earth and heaven in full semantic propriety. It limbs itself as we please. Its parts are "condense or rare," enfolding the entirety with no loss in local concentration. It varies its body at will, dilating fact into metaphor and reintegrating metaphor into fact. It flies. And to these graces of angelic corporeality—fineness, substantiality, plasticity, flight—we must not fail to add the immortality it strives for, successfully up to now. Fame was not, at last, an infirmity of noble mind, but a mental body of unfallen vitalities.

Milton wished for more than an immortality of fame. Like all Christians, he wished for immortality. But he wanted immortality in a particular and heterodox universe. The orthodox may expect the resurrection of the body, but Milton went much further in stipulating the materiality of the hereafter. Miltonic man, in a sense, *does* live by bread alone; in heaven as on earth, he will eat, and he will exercise the rest of his senses as well. For the divided and distinguished worlds of Christian orthodoxy Milton substituted a graded continuum by which we climb the scale to heaven. There is no otherness beyond the solidity of matter, only degrees of solidity. One inalienable characteristic of this universe is its tangibility, and the tangible to a blind man—the respiration of air, the taste and weight and internal companionship of food, the coordinates of known objects—must constitute the real more concertedly than it does for the sighted. We are told by the "So much the rather" of the invocation to light that "To see and tell" of the invisible transcendent realm will compensate our poet for his lost perception. "And so," Masson wrote [in his seven-volume *Life of Milton*], "his very blindness . . . assisting him in his stupendous task, by having already converted all external space in his own sensations into an infinite globe of circumambient blackness or darkness through which he could dash brilliance at his pleasure, there did come forth a cosmical epic which was without a precedent and remains without a parallel." By creating *en image* the cosmos of *Paradise Lost,* Milton filled the emptiness of his "darkness visible" with masses, colors, and motions. He was insistent about the possible actuality of this compensatory world of images; no echelon of Miltonic being is in principle unimaginable. In the most famous critique of this emphatic imagining, Samuel Johnson directs us to the right point in coming to the wrong conclusion:

> Another inconvenience of Milton's design is, that it requires the description of what cannot be described, the agency of spirits. He saw that immateriality supplied no images, and that he could not show angels acting but by instruments of action; he therefore invested them with form and matter. This, being necessary, was therefore defensible; and he should have secured the consistency of his system, by keeping immateriality out of sight, and enticing his reader to drop it from his thoughts. But he has unhappily perplexed his poetry with his philosophy.

Johnson assumed that Milton believed in the immateriality of the spirit world, but his mistake reveals one of the reasons Milton opposed this belief. On the "universal blanc" of his sightlessness the poet imagined a phenomenal heaven. Were he an orthodox imaginer, he would have assumed, as orthodox Johnson assumed, "that immateriality supplied no images." But if his compensatory images signified an orthodox heaven, whose authentic mode of being was unimaginable because extraphenomenal, then in the process of understanding them their solidity would have to be dissolved back into the very emptiness Milton had contracted to escape from. The sublime creations of an orthodox Milton would, in the end, have replicated the "blanc" they were intended to cancel.

Christianity often projects as the great object of our desire an impalpable and foodless world. But this empty idealist heaven held no reward for blind Milton. The dream visitation of his veiled wife in Sonnet 23 appears "such, as yet once more I trust to have / Full sight of her in Heaven without restraint"—and in the universe designed for *Paradise Lost*, full hearing, full smell, full touch, full taste. Milton had experienced the impoverishment of mere mentality. Having dropped into a state resembling pure mind, he came to discover profound reassurance in the abiding presence of material things. Monism in this respect was a guardian philosophy, guaranteeing the steadfastness of this world by locating redemption within it. A mature mind may decide with good reason that "he has unhappily perplexed his poetry with his philosophy," and find amusement in those sad fragments of Renaissance hermeticism that Milton collected together to lend this philosophy its poignantly vulnerable credibility. I reply that heavens, whatever we must accomplish to reach them, exist essentially to be desired. Do not some of our most disorienting fantasies cast us into a fearful combination of blindness and immateriality? Wherever one might go in the monist universe of *Paradise Lost*, he would always be in touch.

The Gender of Milton's Muse and the Problem of the Fit Reader

Maureen Quilligan

If we . . . look at one of Milton's invocations in *Paradise Lost*, we shall see how he confronts the problems of the gender of inspiration and the concomitant problem of his reader's gender. In book 7 Milton invokes his muse for the first time by a specific name—Urania—and for the first time explicitly indicates that the Muse can be figured forth as female in gender. (In book 1, Milton invokes a double-gendered Spirit, who "with mighty wings outspread / Dove-like sat'st brooding on the vast abyss / And madest it pregnant" (1.20–22). The Invocation to book 3, insofar as it associates the Holy Light with the Son/sun (potentially distinct from the Muse), would appear to address a more specifically masculine source of inspiration. However, guessing the genders to the first two invocations is not as important as sensing the peculiar impact of Milton's directly assigning one in book 7.) Embedded within this invocation is Milton's most famous remark about his readership; it is important to look closely at the interconnections between the source of his inspiration and his fears about his audience. After naming Urania, he makes a request:

> Return me to my native element:
> Lest from this flying steed unreined, (as once
> Bellerophon, though from a lower clime)
> Dismounted, on the Aleian field I fall
> Erroneous there to wander and forlorn.

From *Milton's Spenser: The Politics of Reading.* © 1983 by Cornell University Press.

Half yet remains unsung, but narrower bound
Within the visible diurnal sphere;
Standing on earth, not rapt above the pole,
More safe I sing with mortal voice, unchanged
To hoarse or mute, though fallen on evil days,
On evil days though fallen, and evil tongues;
In darkness, and with dangers compassed round,
And solitude; yet not alone, while thou
Visit'st my slumbers nightly, or when morn
Purples the east: still govern thou my song,
Urania, and fit audience find, though few.

(7.16–31)

There is a special relevance to the gender of the Muse in book 7, for
the book sings the story of creation, of the birth of the earth, the poet's
"native" element, in terms of a cosmic femaleness: the earth is female,
the light itself is female, the waters themselves a womb, and out of
earth's womb come all the other creatures—so that on the sixth day
"earth in her rich attire / Consummate lovely smiled" (lines 501–2).
Out of a female entity comes a male creature and then a female: thus
the female light is born before the male sun, whose light is refracted by
the female moon, and the female earth gives birth to the two gendered
animals. Only with the creation of Adam is this pattern reversed:

Male he created thee, but thy consort
Female for race;

(7.529–30)

In the first two invocations, the poet asks for aid in singing his song
and for protection against the dangerous ineffabilities he courts in its
very singing; in book 7 Milton turns to consider the dangers posed
him by his audience. The danger is posed by a force that is, like the
inspirational source, peculiarly female:

But drive far off the barbarous dissonance
Of Bacchus and his revellers, the race
Of that wild rout that tore the Thracian bard
In Rhodope, where woods and rocks had ears
To rapture, till the savage clamour drowned
Both harp and voice; nor could the Muse defend
Her son. So fail not thou, who thee implores:
For thou art heavenly, she an empty dream.

(7.32–39)

Of course those who tore Orpheus limb from limb were women, maenads who in the midst of their frenzied worship of Dionysus were themselves inspired by a god. As Ovid tells the story, the women attack Orpheus because they think that he despises them:

> So with his singing Orpheus drew the trees,
> The beasts, the stones, to follow, when, behold!
> The mad Ciconian women, fleeces flung
> Across their maddened breasts, caught sight of him
> From a near hill-top, as he joined his song
> To the lyre's music. One of them, her tresses
> Streaming in the light air, cried out: "Look there!
> There is our despiser!" and she flung a spear
> Straight at the singing mouth, but the leafy wand
> Made only a mark and did no harm. Another
> Let fly a stone, which, even as it flew
> Was conquered by the sweet harmonious music,
> Fell at his feet, as if to ask for pardon.
>
> (Humphries, trans., 11.1–13)

Orpheus's music might have made him safe, but the maenads' own cacophanous music drowns Orpheus's in "savage clamour," and the woods and rocks, at first his worshipers, become the weapons of his death.

This compelling story obviously bothered Milton profoundly; he refers to it in "L'Allegro"—where Eurydice is only half-won and another music may please Pluto more; he refers to it again in *Lycidas*, where Milton first asks the question he answers in *Paradise Lost* by calling Calliope an "empty dream":

> What could the muse herself that Orpheus bore,
> The muse for her enchanting son
> Whom universal nature did lament,
> When by the rout that made the hideous roar,
> His gory visage down the stream was sent,
> Down the swift Hebrus to the Lesbian shore.
>
> (lines 58–63)

The fear of dismemberment so startling in these passages (like the dismemberment written out of *The Faerie Queene* by Spenser's revisions of Ovid), stresses the very vulnerability of the poet in his inspiration. The maenads not only destroyed a great and inspired poet, they destroyed an exemplary husband, who had descended to hell to retrieve his dead wife; as such they are incalculably central to Milton's own problems in writing *Paradise Lost*. The barbarous dissonance of Bacchus and his revelers stand for any readers who read without the proper inspiration that is implied by Urania's rendering them "fit" (though few). Yet we should not dismember the poem's relationship to its Ovidian text here and ignore the undeniable sexual conflict played out in its verses.

To image inspiration itself as female is no threat to Milton: his own muse is a protectress. But the inspiration *of* females—themselves inspired votaries of a god—is; we would do well to ask why. Milton would have known that Dionysus/Bacchus was not merely a wine-besotted drunkard, but a Comus-like god of the earth's fertility and therefore an especially appropriate pagan god to call up and cast out of his account of Hebrew creation. Insofar as the maenads share, however parodically and demonically, in the intimacy of relations between divine power and human song, Milton casts out a type of inspiration at the same time that he casts out a type of reader. His casting-out is, finally, crucially political, and we should consider for a moment how unfashionable and politically suspect the kind of inspiration Milton claimed for himself was in mid-seventeenth-century England.

The anonymous author of *An Answer* to the *Doctrine and Discipline of Divorce* had taxed Milton with antinomianism:

> We answer: this is a wilde, mad, and frantick divinitie, just like to the opinions of the Maids of Algate; Oh say they, we live in Christ, and Christ doth all for us; we are Christed with Christ and Godded with God, and at the same time we sin here, we joyned to Christ do justice in him, for our life is hid with God in Christ.

Milton's answer to this point in *Colasterion* was a witheringly gallant, "the Maids of Algate, whom he flouts, are likely to have more witt then the Servingman at Addlegate." The principles on which Milton wrote the divorce tracts are not so free as the principles upon which he wrote *The Christian Doctrine* (where individual inspiration is to be trusted before the letter of scripture); but that the anonymous author could tax him with a frenzied female antinomianism suggests the real intellectual danger posed by his own understanding of divine inspiration.

Another famous seventeenth-century antinomian, Anne Hutchinson, had not understood the mediate position in which she had been placed simply by being born a woman. If the soul before God had no sex, then why should not women—like maenads—have direct inspired relations with the divinity and be listened to in their interpretations of scripture, equally with their husbands? In 1666 Quaker Margaret Fell had written and published an argument in favor of the ministry of women, titled *Women Speaking Justified, Proved, and Allowed of by the Scriptures*. Christopher Hill quotes two contradictory remarks by her fellow Quaker George Fox about the subjection of women. In the earlier remark, Fox flatly states that he would "suffer not a woman to teach nor usurp authority over the man, but to be silent. . . . If they will learn anything, let them ask their husbands at home." The later remark in 1680 shows qualified support of women: "Neither did God set the man over the woman whilst they kept the image of God and obeyed his voice." As Hill remarks, "between the two statements I have quoted, Fox had himself married." (It was Margaret Fell whom he married.)

As the example of Anne Hutchinson suggests, the history of Protestantism is in part the history of controlling the expectations it raised in women. A telling point made by the anonymous *Answer* to Milton's first divorce tract was that Milton's position allowed women the same freedom as men had to divorce for incompatibility. In the later *Tetrachordon* Milton even went so far as to allow the woman to rule the man, if she were in fact his natural superior: for then "a superior and more natural law comes in, that the wiser should govern the less wise, whether male or female."

Against these startling and sweeping freedoms, Milton places the originary law:

> He for God only, she for God in him.

What is perhaps less immediately striking, but more profoundly interesting (in the context of Milton's sense of his inspiration) is that in this arrangement of the wife's subjection to her husband there is established not only a sexual hierarchy, but a mediated position for the woman with respect to the divine source. *It negates a direct relationship between God and woman.* She is "covered" by her husband, the male, and it is only through him that she may experience the divine. The purpose of her existence is to know divinity, but only mediately, through the darkened glass of her husband's divinity within.

The reasons for this choice (Fox at least had taken a different stand on Eve's status in paradise) are understandable in terms of the social history of seventeenth-century England. If each believer had become his own priest, and was no longer a member of an institutionally visible church, this priest found his congregation shrunk to the literal foundation upon which Paul had based his metaphoric description of Christ's relationship to his church: the love of a husband for his wife. The monarchial state had also dissolved, to be reconstituted anew but without the divine sanctions so successfully promulgated by Elizabeth and so unsuccessfully by the Stuarts. Radical Protestants were thrown back on the one social unit that might still stand—the nuclear family. The intense pressures on this unit required new political emphases, and the stress of Puritan theology, while it looks like a fostering of woman's status, actually puts her—as Milton does—in a more mediated position. As Lawrence Stone points out, "one of the first results of the doctrine of holy matrimony was a strengthening of the authority of the husband over the wife, and an increased readiness of the latter to submit herself to the dictates of the former. . . . This is similar to the paradox by which the first result of an increased concern for children was a greater determination to crush their sinful wills by whipping them" (*The Family, Sex, and Marriage in England, 1500–1800*).

Such is the chicken-and-egg problem of social change that it is also a distinct possibility that the need to reorient the family along stricter hierarchical lines was a cause of the doctrine of holy matrimony, not merely its result. Increasing the authority of the husband over the wife is a conservative social move designed to act as a safety valve on the revolutionary energies unleashed by the Reformation: if there were to be no more bishops and no more kings, there were still to be, finally and irrevocably, patriarchs. Smaller their kingdoms than before, but patriarchies nonetheless.

For a woman to have inspiration directly from God would be to threaten the last hierarchical relationship left; she would thereby have the authority to challenge her husband. By purging his audience of bacchantic revelers Milton purges the disordered unreason of anyone who would not be a fit reader. But taken in its Ovidian context, Milton is purging the maenad female reader who insists on a more direct relationship of her own to divine inspiration. This may seem needlessly to narrow the definition of the unfit—doubtless many more readers than frenzied Protestant prophetesses actually belong in that number. But it usefully indicates the place where Milton draws the line between his traditional, masculine poetic inspiration—at the end of a long line of both pagan and Hebrew prophets—and the newer enthusiasms in which women could legitimately participate (and for which Milton has some Protestant political sympathies). It distinguishes the works of inspiration—some are true vocations, others are not.

The casting out of the maenad reader also usefully suggests where Milton's female reader, reading as a female, must place herself. To be a fit reader, the woman must accept a mediated, covered position, must freely choose to conform to the hierarchy. The hierarchical arrangement is flatly stated; it is not something Milton argues. The arrangement holds by divine fiat (rather like "die he or justice must"); and to "justify" God's ways to woman is not to explain the situation, but to make her choose to accept it. The entire pressure of the argument of *Paradise Lost* as directed at this "covered" female reader is for her freely to choose the mediated position and to accept its rewards with gratitude. And the poem most persuasively holds that there are rewards, rewards as great, in fact, as the rewards held out for man's acceptance of Christ to which they have from the time of Paul been an analogue. Adam chooses to die for love of Eve. Christ chooses to die for love of man. The first choice is wrong and the second is right: but they are both based in love. And one may heretically suspect that Adam's offered sacrifice derives from the divinity within him for which Eve was made.

Milton's Coy Eve: *Paradise Lost* and Renaissance Love Poetry

William Kerrigan and Gordon Braden

The various tradition of the love lyric is among the distinctive contributions of the Renaissance to our literary culture. In no subsequent period will love be the dominant preoccupation of lyric poetry, or would-be poets feel compelled, as a public demonstration of their seriousness, to animate the conventions of literary love. Few Renaissance careers, on the other hand, are without some episode of Petrarchism; and the long arc of that tradition, from the sequences of frustrated or ideal love to the Ovidian consummations of the seventeenth century, comes down on the work of Milton.

Love in the 1645 *Poems* is in certain obvious ways subordinate to the theme of male friendship. Yet if Milton's Italian *diva* was not, after all, such an inspiration, his brief Petrarchan fever signals the future—another of the youthful possibilities reworked triumphantly in *Paradise Lost,* the first and last epic since the *Odyssey* able to render its love story both genuine and positively heroic. The epic centers in a marriage. Its explorations of cosmic space and time invariably return to this proving ground. Satan, God, Christ, angels, freedom, pleasure, work, the Fall, death, grace, inspiration, redemption: everything in this lofty poem gets placed in the history of Adam and Eve's "wedded love." In the end its entire wisdom has been assimilated in their clasped hands, again together on the guided quest for a new bower.

Critics have recognized that Milton uses the narrative positions opened to him during the course of his "great Argument" to evoke

From *ELH* 53, no. 1 (Spring 1986) © 1986 by the Johns Hopkins University Press.

varieties of poetic love, making literary conventions into moral revelations. Thus the famous lyric hailing "wedded love" at the close of
book 4 offers the epithalamion as the speech act appropriate to the first
instance of human love, and this "elect" genre is often contrasted with
the supposedly "Cavalier" seductions of the devil's early speeches to
Eve in book 9, which isolate for praise her singularity while denigrat-
ing her "wedded" relationship. But we want to argue that Milton's
agon with love poetry is considerably richer and more extensive than
these familiar observations suggest. His epic stands as the consummate
expression of the love tradition, at once a monument to its wisdom and
a telling commentary on its treacheries. First, then, we must take a
fresh look at this tradition and the form in which it reached Milton.

Ovid Reborn, Petrarch Revealed

Seventeenth-century love poetry has sometimes been viewed as a
more or less libertine, Ovidian refutation of the Petrarchism that,
imported by Wyatt and Surrey, flourished widely under Elizabeth.
This is true enough, so far as it goes. Marlowe, Ovid's translator, does
indeed cross some threshold when the lovers at the end of *Hero and
Leander* manage to get out of their weird Petrarchan outfits and into
real sexual consummation. Initially overcome with shame, Hero resists
"Like chaste Diana when Acteon spied her" (2.261). But this chased
Diana learns new ways, and learns them, in a magnificent play upon
the same and the different, when practicing the old. Push having come
to shove, she tries to repel the ungoverned Leander. But in the very
rhythm of this resistance—his onslaught prompting her repulsion, her
repulsion prompting his onslaught—Hero discovers nature's way. She
slips into something more comfortable:

> She trembling strove; this strife of hers (like that
> Which made the world) another world begat
> Of unknown joy.
>
> (2.291–93)

From the perspective of literary history, one of the worlds of unknown
joy begotten here is that of consummated English love poetry—the
verse of Donne, Carew, Suckling, Randolph, Lovelace, and Marvell
among others.

Petrarchan conventions, though there were attempts to adapt them
to fulfilled and mutual love (as in Spenser), are clearly most at home

with unconsummated and unrequited love. It is the denying mistress who burns like ice, like fire. It is the denied lover, charged with forgetfulness, who seeks to occlude his hopelessness. When the lady consents, other conventions become appropriate—the epithalamic or the libertine—and these are in fact prominent in the seventeenth century. But several aspects of this last phase of the love tradition retain strong continuity with the Petrarchan wellsprings. In particular, there is a new clarity about the deep logic of Petrarchism, as if the later poets, inhabiting a brave new world of sexual success, could understand the peculiar alliances among love, fame, and poetry that their predecessors negotiated, somewhat blindly, in the grip of their frustration.

The poems in the *Canzoniere* manifest at every turn the resourcefulness of obsession. They appear in the beloved's absence. Fantasy is not only their element, but often their subject—the image of Laura, the memory of Laura, the replaying of her ambiguous gestures in the act of interpreting Laura. This cultivated obsession is petrifying, toxic, shameful, counter to worldly, moral, and religious self-interest. But— and this becomes one of the defining gestures of the Petrarchan tradition—the love is nonetheless to be affirmed as an ideal. The interpretations of Laura must in the end confirm the good sense of her devotee: being herself ideal, she will eventually reward his service to this truth; somehow or other, hope keeps springing up from apparently absolute despair. However we assess their artistic worth, the much-maligned idealizing couplets in the bulk of Shakespeare's sonnets (57: "So true a fool is love that in your will, / Though you do anything, he thinks no ill") should be taken as assertions of genre, submissions to the fundamental rule of idealization, just as the concluding sonnets of self-reproach (152: "For I have sworn thee fair: more perjured eye, / To swear against the truth so foul a lie") should be understood as indictments of Petrarchan rule-following. If we cut away the two trivial Cupid sonnets, Shakespeare's sequence ends with the explosion of its own genre. This, too, like *Hero and Leander,* is one of those thresholds at which literary historians may view the future becoming possible.

One thing the Petrarchan lover has, in compensation for his agony, is poems. In the *Secretum* Laura and poetic fame are as close as the twin sins of lust and pride, but there, as in the *Canzoniere,* literary immortality serves only obliquely to reward the lover's suffering: for Petrarch the laurel in Laura was not an offset. As the tradition developed, however, we do indeed find the sort of calculation that Petrarch would probably have reached had he not been so invested in the *Africa*. Some of the most grandiose claims for the vivifying power of litera- ture in all the Renaissance—the great age of this claim—occur in love lyrics. Petrarch wrote of the worth and steadfastness of his devotion. Subsequent poets, declaring and deploying the equation between love and fame implicit in Petrarch, counted fame-making among their prime worthinesses, as the posthumous fate of Petrarch's own reputa- tion enlarged their capital. Immortal celebrity can be straightforwardly seductive (I alone among my rivals can make you immortal) or threat- eningly seductive (Be kind, or I will betray your cruelty to aftertimes). When artistic immortality rebounds from the lady to the poet himself, it can be simply compensatory, as in Drayton's

> Proudly thou scorn'st my world-out-wearing rhymes,
> And murder'st virtue with the coy disdain:
> And though in youth, my youth untimely perish,
> To keep thee from oblivion and the grave,
> Ensuing ages yet my rhymes shall cherish,
> Where I entomb'd, my better part shall save;
>> And though this earthly body fade and die,
>> My name shall mount upon eternity.
>
> (*Idea* 44)

Shakespeare, Daniel, and Drayton, whose art came to maturity in the golden period of the first wave of English love poetry, leave the impression that their varied deployment of fame arose in the midst of serious disappointment. In seventeenth-century verse the moves in the game seem to be known in advance. The Carew of "Ungrateful Beauty Threatened" tells a Petrarchan mistress that there is something in this situation that she has not considered with sufficient care; she's refusing, it must be remembered, a *poet*. Waller, in his "Story of Phoebus and Daphne, Applied," presents a grieving youth whose complaints fail to win Saccharissa, that artificial sweetener. No cause for lamentation, since the instrumentality of love poetry, despite appearances, is no longer aimed at the stubborn beloved:

> Yet what he sung in his immortal strain,
> Though unsuccessful, was not sung in vain;
> All, but the nymph that should redress his wrong,
> Attend his passion, and approve his song.
> Like Phoebus thus, acquiring unsought praise,
> He catched at love, and filled his arm with bays.

"Apollo," in other words, "hunted Daphne so, / Only that she might laurel grow." Had Waller written this couplet, it would mean that approving readers can stand in for an immune nymph. Embracing an armful of bays, the poet can do without the woman. The solitary egoism of Waller's love poet moves Petrarchism toward the hyperbolic solitude of "The Garden," whose speaker takes the divestment a step further by sacrificing not just the woman but the ambition to wear the laurel, finding his compensation in the radically internal crown of "a green thought in a green shade."

Milton's Italian *Canzone* is also aware in the seventeenth-century manner that Petrarchan verse aims finally at the poet's own fame. Young people of both sexes ask the lovestruck Milton why he is writing in Italian; on another and English river, they assure him, "the immortal guerdon, the crown of unfading leaves, is already sprouting for your head." The crown, *L'immortal guiderdon d'eterne frondi,* is the thing poets would pluck, as even laymen realize. This nexus of love, fame, and crown reappears in the first movement of *Lycidas:*

> Were it not better done as others use,
> To sport with Amaryllis in the shade,
> Or with the tangles of Neaera's hair?
> Fame is the spur that the clear spirit doth raise
> (That last infirmity of noble mind)
> To scorn delights, and live laborious days;
> But the fair guerdon when we hope to find,
> And think to burst out into sudden blaze,
> Comes the blind Fury with th'abhorred shears,
> And slits the thin-spun life. But not the praise,
> Phoebus replied, and touched my trembling ears;
> Fame is no plant that grows on mortal soil
>
> (lines 67–78)

Here again fame compensates for denied love. But in Milton successful desire and poetic immortality have fallen into perfect opposition. Instead of seeking the first and making do with the second, like the wooer of Saccharissa, the clear spirits of *Lycidas* choose fame from the very beginning, and do not woo anybody. The furies that conventionally torment unrequited lovers of Petrarchan verse now strike against the lust for fame; unrequited fame, not love, is the cruelty that must be interpreted in the first third of *Lycidas.* Whereas Petrarch and his followers, like the *stilnovisti* before them, had often negotiated with the unbearable injustice of their frustrated love by projecting their reward into the afterlife, Milton enacts this strategem for the sake of protecting the experience of being famous rather than being loved. This *translatio*, informed by the new awareness of seventeenth-century poetry, retains the key image of the Petrarchan tradition. For Milton's "fair guerdon" almost certainly means "laurel crown," an interpretation that links this passage to the opening line of the elegy, and makes good sense of the first words of Phoebus, whose frustrated desire produced the original laurel crown: "Fame is *no plant* that grows on mortal soil." The knot of love, fame, and crown is rewoven, as we will see, in *Paradise Lost*.

OVID REVEALED, PETRARCH REBORN

Another thing the Petrarchan lover has in compensation for his suffering is the beloved's image. Precisely as in the case of fame, the sacrifice of full presence, of realized sexuality, can have its pleasures. Once again, the psychological transaction by which the image becomes preferable to the woman herself is only latent in Petrarch, but emerges openly in the tradition he inspired. An important English poem for the study of this emergence is "Absence, hear thou my protestation," generally assigned to John Hoskyns, though sometimes attributed to Donne (the more likely choice, judging solely on the basis of its excellence and the Donnean lurch of its sense at the conclusion):

> By absence this good means I gain,
>   That I can catch her
>   Where none can watch her,
>
> In some close corner of my brain;
>   There I embrace and kiss her,
>   And so I both enjoy and miss her.

The mind's a fine and private place, and some, we think, do there embrace. The logic of this consolation reaches a characteristically seventeenth-century finality in a poem like Lovelace's "Love Made in the First Age: To Chloris," where the speaker vengefully rejects the invitation of a woman who once scorned him, preferring instead the joy of ravishing her image: "Crowned with mine own soft beams, / Enjoying of myself I lie." In the solitary enjoyment of his own crowning sunbeams, this Apollo has no interest in external Lauras or laurels. Via this pronounced tendency to replace the woman with her image, the high-minded, idealized sufferings of Petrarchan poetry made a bizarre marriage with the new libertine strands of the seventeenth century.

Libertine poetry is of course dead set, programmatically, against Petrarchism—"whining poetry," as Donne sneered. In his libertine verse Donne promotes a world where honor is but a hymen, and exclusive, jealous devotion is impossible. The indifferent can love her and her, and you and you, *provided that* she be not true, or in other words, that she be herself indifferent: save for the few heretics doomed to be true to faithless lovers, the situation that generates Petrarchism will pass from the earth. Along with attacks on the varieties of female refusal (honor, discretion, coyness), we find in the libertine tradition self-help poems such as Suckling's "Why so pale and wan." Here the Petrarchan convention of supplying hopeful interpretations of ambiguous gestures is turned against the tradition. The speaker's arch assumption that the pale silence of the Petrarchan loser must be a stratagem designed to convert his mistress, and as such sure to fail, neatly reinstalls self-interest as the true ideal; and the lyric ends by detaching the lover from his unobtainable object: "Nothing can make her, / The devil take her." This plank in the libertine platform received extensive support from an unlikely quarter—Burton's blistering pages on "Remedies of Love": "she is lovely, fair, well-favoured, well qualified, courteous and kind: But if she be not so to me, what care I how kind she be? I say with Philostratus, beautiful to others, she is a tyrant to me, and so let her go (*The Anatomy of Melancholy*). Burton proposes numerous exercises to cool passion's heat, among them the deliberate manipulation of the beloved's image so as to produce revulsion. These currents in the libertine tradition, with their pious antecedents in patristic literature, left their mark on *Paradise Lost*. Milton's brief evocation of the "serenade, which the starved lover sings / To his proud fair, best quitted with disdain" (4.769–70) is virtually an epitome of Suckling's "Why so pale and wan." Burton's renewed concern with the self-interested use of repulsive images can be discerned in Raphael's suggestion that Adam cure his uxoriousness by realizing that the rites he values are no more than those enjoyed by copulating animals (8.579–85).

Petrarchism may well be, remembering a Miltonic phrase in Donne's "The Ecstasy," a defect of loneliness. But it is remarkable that so many of the seventeenth-century love poets encountered defects of union. A hangover of postcoital depression awaited them in the new subject matter of sexual success. Ovid as literary master was not the mere inverse of Petrarch. In libertine poetry, the old moral and theological critique of sexual love reappears at the level of nature: there is a curse or privation in the very design of it. As Donne recorded in his "Farewell to Love," sexual consummation is short, depleting, dulling. Jonson lends his authority to this estimate through his translation of *Foeda est in coitu et brevis voluptas,* believed in the Renaissance to be the work of Petronius: "Doing, a filthy pleasure is, and short; / And done, we straight repent us of the sport." Man dislikes an unsolvable problem, and today we have whole industries and professions, products and gurus, devoted to the rectification of these related and design flaws. Seventeenth-century poetry also teems with advice on this matter. Petronius, in Jonson's translation, offered this pregnant suggestion:

> Let us together closely lie, and kiss,
> There is no labour, nor no shame in this;
> This hath pleased, doth please, and long will please; never
> Can this decay, but is beginning ever.

Shameless, endlessly renewable, the kiss is the most innocent of all sexual acts, and avoids almost entirely that sense of decay and death so deeply embedded, linguistically and emotionally, in typical Renaissance descriptions of intercourse. It was probably from following this advice, backed up by several notably delicious kisses elsewhere in Jonson's songs and lyrics, that Robert Herrick became the monarch of osculation in seventeenth-century poetry.

Antifruition was a libertine topos. Some of these *paradossi,* such as Cowley's "Against Fruition," appear to be exercises on a set theme. Others bespeak an actual discipline, a program for chastening the sexual drive by confining it to fantasy. One supposes that Bishop King, the master elegist, lived chastely in a continued marriage to his deceased wife. His "Paradox. That Fruition Destroys Love" delivers the usual complaints. Coition degrades love to lust, and causes the lover to devalue his partner; guilt is its inevitable sequel. The alternative is "expectation and delay":

> Give me long dreams and visions of content,
> Rather than pleasures in a minute spent.
> And since I know before, the shedding rose
> In that same instant doth her sweetness lose,

Upon the virgin-stock still let her dwell
For me to feast my longings with her smell.

This resolve to leave the rosebuds ungathered, to live with unfulfillable images of fulfillment, supplies a regimen for the flesh comparable to the deliberate schemes of image manipulation recommended by Catholics and Protestants alike for the devotional life of the soul. We are once again reminded of Herrick. Like Ovid and Martial, Herrick tells us that "Jocund his Muse was, but his life was chaste," yet the many instances of interrupted or blocked fruition in his lyrics give us better reason to believe the Renaissance poet. Sir Thomas Browne was not the only seventeenth-century male who "could be content that we might procreate like trees, without conjunction, or that there were any way to perpetuate the world without this trivial and vulgar way of coition." (*Religio Medici*). But, Suckling wrote, disposing of Browne's objection, "since there are enough / Born to the drudgery, what need we plough?" The restriction of sexuality to fantasy produced its own issue—brainchildren, poems of indulged erotic imagination. *Hesperides* may be the fullest record we possess of the actual practice of poetic sexual fantasy as programmatic chastity.

Suckling wrote two poems entitled "Against Fruition," and the better of them, "Stay here fond youth and ask no more, be wise," was taken seriously enough to inspire at least two answers, by Edmund Waller and the aptly named Henry Bold. The Suckling lyrics have a somewhat different tone from the ones discussed thus far. Orgasmic disappointment is inexorable—the incarnation of our fallen condition, our severance from heaven. Beneath the jauntiness of the poems lies a conviction that the mind may be, tragically, the best bower we know in this world. " 'Tis expectation makes a blessing dear: / It were not heaven, if we knew what it were." Having is finite, summed, just what it is: a score. Anticipation, on the other hand, is untold, incalculable, forever beckoning, and above all preserves the love object from debasement. The answers by Waller and Bold respond to the self-defeating silliness of the wormseed advice that Suckling pours on the tail of his fond youth. If sex is not, as Browne declared, "the foolishest act a wise man commits," it is certainly the subject about which wise men are given to speak most foolishly. So, Bold replies, "Go on, bold boy! and put her to't, be wise!"

Yet the poems deserves a more reflective reply. In Suckling's hands this topos loses its oddity and reveals its stalwart allegiance to

Petrarchism: at stake in the antifruition poems is the preservation of an ideal; they are obedient, in a libertine setting, to the fundamental rule of the Petrarchan tradition. The second of Suckling's efforts, "Fie upon hearts that burn with mutual fire," inverts *carpe diem* by urging the mistress to be coy and unforthcoming, and systematically unmakes the world projected in Donne's "The Indifferent" by demanding that the sexual passions of men and women never be in sync. After decades of poetic assaults on Petrarchan love, Suckling here reinvents from libertine premises the Petrarchan mistress, and for the sake of ideal sexual pleasure teaches to seventeenth-century beloveds the old virtue of coyness. Rochester, no less, was alive to the fleshy compensations of this proposal. His lyric "The Platonic Lady" shows us an antifruitional mistress laying down her rules, improving upon the usual advice of the topos by substituting infinite foreplay for infinite fantasy:

> I hate the thing is called enjoyment:
> Besides it is a dull employment,
> It cuts off all that's life and fire
> From that which may be termed desire;
>
> .   .   .   .
>
> I love a youth will give me leave
> His body in my arms to wreathe;
> To press him gently, and to kiss;
> To sigh, and look with eyes that wish
>
> .   .   .   .
>
> I'd give him liberty to toy
> And play with me, and count it joy.
> Our freedom should be full complete,
> And nothing wanting but the feat.

To this day, such advice has its practitioners. But the profoundest answer to Suckling, or at least to the questions he raises for lovers, was given by Andrew Marvell. "To His Coy Mistress" opens with an infinite courtship, which is then rejected by a frantic doing in which the very shortness or hurriedness of the sexual act, the complaint of so many poet-lovers of the century, becomes precisely its *excellence* in our fallen race with time.

The need to master the faults and privations at the heart of our sexuality is everywhere at issue in libertine poetry. These authors want to ensure the renewability, the unending fascination, of sexual love. A bedrock fear of "aphanisis"—the term Ernest Jones coined for the disappearance of sexual desire—drives this literature. Nothing is forbidden in Carew's "A Rapture" except disinterest: "We only sin when Love's rites are not done." The initial attack on honor in this fine and revealing poem is one of several indicators that seduction or acceptance, sexual connection for the first time, is no longer the major focus of literary love. The exhilarating first times of *Hero and Leander* or Donne's elegy "On his Mistress Going to Bed" are a generation away; the problem now is how to "die and rise *the same*," without deflating desire or its object, ready to die and rise again. "A Rapture" begins in imitation of Donne's elegy, but where Donne leaves off, Carew takes off—and then takes off again. The sexual act most elaborately described in the poem is the *second* time. Carew's lyrics often end with comebacks and renewals, and he left us, appropriately enough, "A Second Rapture." Restoration, provision, prevenient secular grace, a warrantee against decaying desire: all the libertine poets crave futurity, and this is the wish that, in a Suckling or a Rochester, revives repressed Petrarchism in a libertine world. The antifruition poems reposition desire on the before side of consummation. With this shift, frustration emerges once again as the ideal: frustration, be thou my pleasure! The topos we have studied imaginatively reclaims the innocence that the first phase of Renaissance love poetry was largely written in the hope of losing.

Before proceeding to explanations, consequences, and *Paradise Lost,* it might be well, following the example of Freud, simply to acknowledge the sheer peculiarity of human sexuality. The reinvention of Petrarchan frustration from Ovidian premises may be an absurd folly, correctly diagnosed by the Bolds of the seventeenth century, but the antifruition topos also concedes an authentic waywardness in our sexual passion. In his essay on "The Most Prevalent Form of Degradation in Erotic Life"—one especially pertinent to the aspects of Renaissance lyric under discussion here—Freud opposes the idea that satisfaction engenders degradation in all the spheres of our desire. Sexual passion and its objects are uniquely fragile:

> But is it also true that with the satisfaction of an instinct its psychical value always falls just as sharply? Consider, for example, the relation of a drinker to wine. Is it not true that wine always provides the drinker with the same toxic satisfaction, which in poetry has so often been compared to erotic satisfaction—a comparison acceptable from the scientific point

of view as well? Has one ever heard of the drinker being obliged constantly to change his drink because he soon grows tired of keeping to the same one? On the contrary, habit constantly tightens the bond between a man and the kind of wine he drinks. Does one ever hear of a drinker who needs to go to a country where wine is dearer or drinking is prohibited, so that by introducing obstacles he can reinforce the dwindling satisfaction that he obtains? Not at all. If we listen to what our great alcoholics, such as Böcklin, say about their relation to wine, it sounds like the most perfect harmony, a model of a happy marriage. Why is the relation of the lover to his sexual object so very different?

It is my belief that, however strange it may sound, we must reckon with the possibility that something in the nature of the sexual instinct itself is unfavourable to the realization of complete satisfaction.

This uncanny passage, which should interest future annotators of Herrick's sack poems, might even serve as a preface to the seventeenth-century secular lyric in its entirety. Freud asks us to reckon with the possibility that complete and unequivocal satisfaction of sexual desire is an impossible attainment. As if in secret agreement with this proposition, we protect desire and its object against mutual disillusionment by erecting obstacles between them. Fantasy, poetry itself, may be among these obstacles. There is something Petrarchan in the nature of us. The barriers we erect to prevent what Milton calls in *Paradise Lost* "Casual fruition" (4.767) are in Freud's view a topos of the unconscious, whose beloveds are images, not realities, and whose ideal is mere desire, not its end in satisfaction.

MILTON MAKES IT RIGHT

Alexander Ross observes that Browne must be wrong about the inherent foolishness of the sexual act, since God himself had sculpted the genitals of man and woman (*Medicus Medicatus*, 1645). *Paradise Lost* is also happy, by and large, with the gift of sexuality: God made it right, following, with certain modifications, a design he had already worked out in the creation of the angels. But like all writing about sexual love, Milton's has a peculiar fantasy structure, a *way* in which sex is right. The crux of Adam and Eve's sexual connection is a cunningly and poetically imagined version of the dominant sexual fantasy of the Renaissance, or if that is too provincial, of the dominant sexual fantasy of Western culture from the Romans to this day, so pervasive and so enmeshed in cultural symbols that to many people it has looked like nature, with little or nothing of the fantastic about it. Moreover, Milton presents this fantasy so as to guard his garden sexuality, not only from hypocrites who feel that this particular beast should not be there, but also from the libertine melancholy that fell so heavily on the love poetry of his day.

In rough and ready form the fantasy, as well as its major metaphors, is already there in Ovid. It is slowed down into a ritual, given rules and a code of minute gestures, by the Christian tradition of courtly love. It is central to Petrarch, who dwells on myths of dangerous chase—the ill fates of Daphne and Actaeon. The fantasy passed down through the centuries is venery—the love hunt. Men chase, women flee. Men aggressively manifest their interest. Women are coy, demur, hard-to-get, which is to say, undeclared, ambiguous. When the fantasy is successfully realized, there comes a turning, a sign from the woman that she will yield by gradual degrees and the two desires will be as one, declared equally and simultaneously in sexual activity—the moment dramatized with such pungency in *Hero and Leander* when turning coincides with doing. The fantasy has its inverse, as when Corinna comes at noon to Ovid or the special lady stalks Wyatt in his chambers. But the impressed male's thankfulness reveals that these gifts are, indeed, breaks with routine.

This is the erotic scenario Milton activates when, outdoing his predecessors, he undertakes the narration of the first first time in the person of Eve. The act is, of course, a double loss of virginity—still considered, in many places, the ideal initiation. Milton's may be the most reflective, even philosophical account of sexual consummation in all of Renaissance literature. For the story of how Eve lost her virginity turns upon the psychological and metaphysical status of her own image. Beginning in primitive form as the captivating shape that pleases in the pool, Eve's image of herself goes through an astonishing series of intellectual metamorphoses, as if Milton were creating a new genre for this occasion—Ovidian wisdom literature. Here is the voice of God breaking into Eve's vain rapture:

> What thou seest,
> What there thou seest fair creature is thyself,
> With thee it came and goes: but follow me,

> And I will bring thee where no shadow stays
> Thy coming, and thy soft embraces, he
> Whose image thou art, him thou shall enjoy
> Inseparably thine, to him shalt bear
> Multitudes like thyself, and thence be called
> Mother of human race.
>
> (4.467–75)

God ends her ignorant and therefore innocent romance with her image by first imparting to her the unmistakably Platonic concept of the mirror image. From this primal idea others are born. The future opens. Eve is held by imaginative foreshadowing to him whose image *she* is, different from the mirror image in that this one can be embraced as a sexual partner. The embrace, the dialectic of the flesh, will disseminate her image in "Multitudes like thyself." In dilating the concept of the image, God has moved from mirror to mother, arriving thereby at the concept of Eve: the voice is reflecting her in a mirror of knowledge. God's speech concludes with the most sophisticated of the images of Eve—what she will be called, "Mother of human race," the definitive epithet forever to be coupled with her proper name.

"Invisibly thus led," self-knowledge being the route to sexual knowledge, Eve sees Adam and the love hunt is off and running. She turns and flees. Adam gives chase. The narrative itself is now mirroring the romance at the pool, when also Eve "started back" and "soon returned." Adam calls out, mirroring the voice of God. But whereas the divine speaker reflected in his invisible mirror the image of Eve, the voice of the male, of "he / Whose image thou art," reflects himself:

> Return fair Eve,
> Whom fly'st thou? Whom thou fly'st, of him thou art,
> His flesh, his bone; to give thee being I lent
> Out of my side to thee, nearest my heart
> Substantial life, to have thee by my side
> Henceforth an individual solace dear;
> Part of my soul I seek thee, and thee claim
> My other half.
>
> (4.482–88)

"Me" is the answer to his initial question, but a "me" whose essence is relatedness to "thee," "My other half." Whereupon her hand is gently seized, and that transition from repulsion to welcome that Marlowe represented in the rocking of the body Milton renders in a play of hands. We are given to know that Eve fled because Adam's body, in its angularity, was "Less winning soft, less amiably mild, / Than that smooth watery image" (lines 479–80). Since she must know at this point that the image was of her own form, Adam's rival in the courtship of Eve is Eve herself.

The narrative ends with a passage commonly subject to misinterpretation:

> I yielded, and from that time see
> How beauty is excelled by manly grace
> And wisdom, which alone is truly fair.
>
> (4.489–91)

She is telling us just what, after all these image lessons, she has been enabled to "see," and there is nothing in her conclusions that need disturb a modern liberal mind. "Manly" modifies "grace," but not "wisdom": wisdom is something separate from manly grace, though joined with it in their shared superiority to physical beauty. Beauty is excelled by manly grace. Eve is simply telling us what her yielding meant, telling us that the male body is preferable as a love object to the more beautiful female body, that Adam is preferable to his rival, that she is, in other words, heterosexual. And beauty is excelled by wisdom, as in the intellectual sense given to the verb "see" in this very passage. Wisdom led her from the beautiful shape in the pool, and again detached her from that image, thus bringing her narrative to "I yielded," when reborn in the invisible voice of Adam calling out behind her. Wisdom, which is linguistic and invisible, conceptual rather than perceptible, is a higher-order beauty, alone *truly* fair, because truth is not an image but a knowing, and for the speaker of these words, was first of all a knowing of a beautiful image. Having told her tale and summed her wisdom, Eve proceeds to act out its happy ending, yielding to Adam and receiving his impregnating kisses.

Man chases, woman yields. When Satan first sees her, Eve has adopted the same erotic attitude she learned in the beginning—subjection, submission, yielding. Drawing out his syntax, Milton seems driven to become more and more precise about the logic of their erotic bond:

> Subjection, but required with gentle sway,
> And by her yielded, by him best received,

> Yielded with coy submission, modest pride,
> And sweet reluctant amorous delay.

>   (4.308–11)

Coy submission—a red flag word in seventeenth-century poetry, and
we are reading, it is well to remember here, Andrew Marvell's em-
ployer. Eve has learned something from those moments in the libertine
tradition that unexpectedly reaffirm the erotic value of modesty and
withholding. In her yielding, there is a pretense of refusal, an evocation
of the Platonic Lady. A fluid coupling of three perfect adjectives
charges the word "delay" with considerable libidinal power. Reluctant
to be amorous? Reluctant to delay? In either case it is sweet. Apparently they play this slowpoke game of chasing and yielding, sweeten-
ing the day, but delay consummation until the night: as at the end of
book 4, sex is the last thing they do, the pleasure that crowns the
working day and discharges the energy built up through sweet reluctant amorous delaying.

A naked man and woman arise in the morning, intermix the
duties of the day with flirtatious venery, then consummate their love at
night with a real capture, a real yielding, and go to sleep. This is
paradise. It depends upon the wise management of temptation. In the
Miltonic temptation the offer, if successfully resisted, will eventually
be given as a reward in a higher and transmuted form. Milton's sexual
imagination was of a piece with his moral vision—patient resistance in
the service of ideal consummation. In the rhythm of paradisal eroticism, as in the rhythm of sacred history, all is "ever best found in the
close" (*Samson Agonistes,* 1748). At our entrance into Eden in *Paradise
Lost* we are introduced, as in the Elizium of Carew's "A Rapture," to
an established sexual relationship. But in place of the voluptuous décor
that ensures sexual renewal in Carew's poem we find instead a drama
of delay in which Adam and Eve restage each day, as reliable foreplay,
the chase-capture-yielding of the first time. As in Milton generally,
origins are conclusive. In his representation of the ideal sexual life,
virginity is always symbolically being lost, and every time is as the
first time. Eve will not, at day's end, turn away, coyer than she is
submissive:

>   nor turned I ween
> Adam from his fair spouse, nor Eve the rites
> Mysterious of connubial love refused.

>   (4.741–43)

The text says that Adam did not turn from Eve, and Eve did not refuse, but it may be lawful to speculate that she might have turned away, as she did in the beginning, only to return in answerable style.

There is something brilliant about even the sexual fantasies of the man. "Sweet reluctant amorous delay" can be viewed as Milton's deft contribution to the ongoing problem of how to enjoy another sexually and not, afterwards, suffer the rebound of degradation—a bulwark against boredom, disinterest, depletion, depression, lovelessness, all of the curses and deprivations that, in libertine literature, constitute sexuality's particular brush with the Fall. Milton understood the erotic importance of the barrier. In his Eden, coyness and delay protect love by incorporating an obstacle into a sexual life of satisfied consummation. Antifruition sets up happy fruition.

That surely was his goal, as can be learned from observing what he has done with the three major myths of the Petrarchan tradition—the love chase of Apollo and Daphne, the disastrous love-at-first-sight of Actaeon and Diana, and the suicidal love of Narcissus: all three myths of nonconsummation, of unfulfilled love and thwarted chase.

Milton subsumes Narcissus and Apollo-Daphne into the narrative of love's happy genesis, incorporating even the myths of the barrier in his representation of fulfillment. There were two threats to the primal mating. Eve might have fixed her eyes forever on the image, but God intervenes to break the Narcissus spell; like Daphne, she might never have consented to capture, but the voice of Adam intervenes to break the Daphne spell. Furthermore, Eve's birth narrative is linked in several ways to Sin's, where the Narcissus myth appears *in malo*. Like Eve, Satan first recoiled from his "perfect image" (2.764), then "Becamest enamoured." Eventually Sin conceived, "such joy" he took with her "in secret" (lines 765–66): we are not told how many times this secret joy occurred, but the most imaginative guess would be only once. For Sin is the prototype of the degraded love object—an unlovable horror when beheld for the first time after fruition. Myths implode upon this victim of decay. Her unchaste, monstrously fertile womb suffers the fate of Actaeon, hounded by her own dogs. Irksome disappointment, pining always in vain desire, is the demonic fate in *Paradise Lost*: Satan, we are told in the hymn to wedded love, "bids abstain" (4.748); inverting the usual vision of the Christian cosmos, this poem shows us sex in Heaven and deprivation in Hell. Implicit in the way Milton has apportioned these major Petrarchan myths among the two love stories of his epic lies a redemptive polemic against frustration.

How it Goes Wrong: Satan, Arch-Petrarchist

Human sexuality does not result in Eve's degradation in the eyes of her husband, but rather the opposite, as he informs Raphael when seeking counsel on this matter in book 8. His problem bears upon the social meaning of the chase and capture fantasy.

There is a charming and suggestive episode in the *Lusiads* of Camoens. At last the long-wandered Portuguese receive a reward from Venus, their divine champion. She peoples an island with her nymphs and instructs them in how to please these storm-tossed sailors. And the game on this Belle Isle, at the wise decree of Venus, is the dominant sexual fantasy of Western culture: the nymphs flee, the sailors run them down. But one sailor, a man notoriously unlucky in love, draws a perverse nymph. She will not be caught. After the other sailors have captured their partners and they have consented to more stationary delights, the unlucky sailor is still in pursuit. Who told you it was me? he cries out in despair, and quotes Petrarch—"What a wall is set between the grain and my hand" (*Canzoniere* 56)—as he is swept to a vision of his fate as a calculus of endless frustration: even if you were to stop now, I would be too tired to touch you (book 9, stanzas 77–78). But he is in fact completing the nymph's erotic playlet; at the sound of his lament she returns to prove him memorably wrong. She is the pupil of Venus, attuned to complaints, that Petrarchans dreamed of finding. She is also, according to Camoens, desirous of selling at a greater price than the others (stanza 76)—a nymph with a high opinion of her worth.

Why must there be a chase? Why must woman run and man pursue even in Eden, even on the Isle of Venus? We have suggested in psychoanalytic terms that obstacles may help to save desire and its object from decay. There is a social side as well to this preservation of value. Venery has to do with dearness, which is how Adam, speaking with his angelic counsellor, interprets the ambiguous gesture of Eve's original flight:

> Yet innocence and virgin modesty,
> Her virtue and the conscience of her worth,
> That would be wooed, and not unsought be won,
> Not obvious, not obtrusive, but retired,
> The more desirable, or to say all,
> Nature her self, though pure of sinful thought,
> Wrought in her so, that seeing me, she turned.
>
> (8.501–7)

Her flight was "more desirable" than overt invitation would have been, but that was not its purpose. As women will tend to do in a society in which they flee and men pursue (Adam, making the common mistake, confuses her behavior with "Nature her self"), Eve was expressing "the conscience of her worth." (At the precise moment she took flight from Adam, Eve may of course have been driven by other motives, such as fear.) By her elusiveness, by the precise degree of her coyness, by exactly how hard she is to get, a woman measures her worth, and by his pursuit, by the precise degree of his tenacity, by exactly the hard effort he expends, a man acknowledges this worth: a match. When a period of delay and not an end in itself, Petrarchan devotion is a way of reckoning or settling female worth. Male worth remains secondary as the game was usually played in Renaissance poetry, determined primarily by the poet-lover's willing consent to his mistress's demand. The hunted leads, the hunter follows. Self-interest—male worth—keeps resurfacing in the characteristic conflicts between reason and passion or the chiding friend and the heedless heart, but must be put aside in obedience to the fundamental rule of idealization. The rule, in this sense, is submission to the female's assessment of her value—the chase at all costs.

After proposing an infinite courtship in the first section of "To His Coy Mistress," Marvell surprisingly adds, contrary to his ironic hyperbole,

> For Lady you deserve this State;
> Nor would I love at lower rate.

Prolonged Petrarchan devotion, about to be repudiated by mortal necessity, retains its imaginative truth. The impossibly lengthy chase required by her coyness is indeed the ideal measure of her value: though in a subjunctive world contrary to mortal fact, the woman is loved at her own rate. Even in the best of the *carpe diem* poems a social transaction, an agreed reckoning of female worth, lies at the heart of the chase and capture fantasy. In *Paradise Lost* this game is fraught with moral danger.

Because sweet reluctant amorous delay will provide a daily reaffirmation of "the conscience of her worth," Adam will inevitably be vulnerable to the opposite of object-debasement. The game that preserves Eve's value from the fate of debasement works all too well, and the consequence is a tendency in the first husband to abase himself before the idol of his mate. It is no surprise when he falls "Fondly overcome with female charm" (9.999). The sexual fantasy Milton embedded at the origins of human love simply has to, by its very meaning, buck against the ordained hierarchy that sets the man over the woman. It makes the Fall explicable.

Eve also falls when fondly overcome with female charm: "nor was godhead from her thought" (9.790). It is not until the fatal temptation of book 9 that we can appreciate why Milton married the origin of love to so many lessons about the image of Eve. At the moral center of the epic stands an acute diagnosis of Renaissance love poetry.

The deadly *venator* in this love hunt is Satan, eavesdropper at the intimate revelations of book 4. He paid special attention, it is clear, to the images that surrounded the loss of virginity. Adam's first words to Eve ("Return fair Eve, / Whom fly'st thou?") appear to have inspired the dream of flight Satan designs for her in order to strengthen that initial mysterious impulse toward solitude; adopting the voice of Adam, who spoke against her romance with her image, he tells her that stars exist to gaze upon her beauty. As the voice of the snake, he leads Eve symbolically back to the image in the pool, Adam's rival, and uncreates her wisdom. The successor to that image is the tree of prohibition in book 9. Satan assures her that its fruits pleased as "the teats / Of ewe or goat dropping with milk at even, / Unsucked of lamb or kid" (lines 581–83). Like Eve, or like the image of Eve he intends to reflect, the tree is an ignored mother, a provider whose worthy goods have not been allowed their due fruition; it is subordinate, underappreciated, cursed. (See Eve's last unfallen musings, 9.745–59: she is addressing herself.) As the snake leaves her, her eyes are once again fixed in self-worship on her own enchanting image; to eat the fruit is to realize or unfold her true worth. And once again, as at the beginning, she has no consciousness that the tree she thinks she knows is in fact her own image. Gone is the wisdom. Gone is the sweet reluctant amorous delay: a rash hand plucks and eats. Twice in the poem Eve has desired solitude. When she departs from the dinnertime symposium, it is for the sake of erotic delay; Adam will intermix his account with "Grateful digression, and solve high dispute / With conjugal caresses, from his lip / Not words alone pleased her" (8.55–57). But in the next book the motive for her solitude includes some sense of oppressive closeness, "so near each other thus all day" (9.220), some souring on the sweet flirtation of their daytime eroticism. Accomplishment is more to her liking: "Looks intervene and smiles" (9.222). As it turns out, delay is one thing, absence another. For the absence of Adam gives Eve over to his rival—the solitude and singularity of her image.

Satan accomplishes his design by exploiting something very close to what seventeenth-century poets learned about the logic of Petrarchism:

> Fairest resemblance of thy maker fair,
> Thee all things living gaze on, all things thine
> By gift, and thy celestial beauty adore
> With ravishment beheld, there best beheld
> Where universally admired; but here
> In this enclosure wild, these beasts among,
> Beholders rude, and shallow to discern
> Half what in thee is fair, one man except,
> Who sees thee? (And what is one?) Who shouldst be seen
> A goddess among gods, adored and served
> By angels numberless, thy daily train.
>
> (9.538–48)

And what is one? Waller's Apollo found in "unsought praise," an armful of laurels, a good trade-off from the lost Daphne. Eve should be adored by many, an empress at a civilized court, crowned and on display. The imperial destiny laid before Eve extricates her image from the exclusive mutual devotion of her love and repositions it as the centerpiece of an empire of gazes, guiding her desire onto the same track that made fame an agreeable substitute for love in the Petrarchan tradition. Fame is the first infirmity of fallen mind: Satan fell when he could not bear to be eclipsed by the crowned son. The Cavalier poets spoke for erotic satisfaction, which was the usual motive for the imperial compliments they paid to women. Satan, a specialist in the pleasures left to the frustrated, draws rather on the imperial yearnings, the wish for the crown, found in Petrarchan love.

Her vulnerability to this lethal gambit springs from the way Milton represented ideal love. The image in the pool was never abandoned. Adam fell in love with it. Eve, still thinking about it, ran away. Adam chased after her, willing to love at whatever rate she priced her worth. Eve yielded, fixing the value of her image, and each day the game has been replayed. Since Miltonic love is ultimately about the determination of female worth, one can readily see how Satan is able to convert Eve from the fixed value agreed upon in her marriage to the inflation of an imperial reckoning. What is one? Love is a fragile knot woven of narcissism—the consummate pleasure of paradise, but equally the precondition of paradise lost. As Eve falls, Adam is weaving "Of choicest flowers a garland to adorn / Her tresses, and her rural labours crown, / As reapers oft are wont their harvest queen" (9.840–42). The bridge between this innocent rural token woven by a husband for his harvest queen and the pomposities of Satan's Hell, where he sits crowned like a king of kings, in Godlike imitated state—the bridge actually built in the poem by Sin and Death—measures exactly the extent to which Eve's image has fallen.

The temptation Eve designs for Adam is a love trial. He must again reckon her worth. And again, eating, he pays the price, choosing against another Eve. Courtly love was charged early on with idolatry, and Adam's Fall is in this sense a medieval one. Eve's is the more modern. In the Petrarchan poetry of the Renaissance the old threat of idolatry gave way to the newly expansive and resourceful ego of the suitor-poet; the rejected male began to try out new and extravagant compensations, the most enduring of these being poetic immortality via an empire of admirers. The female Fall has this distinctly Renaissance tone. Hell in *Paradise Lost,* built like Renaissance civilization itself in imitation of a lost magnificence, smacks of Burckhardt's Renaissance, with its great building remembered from Milton's Italian travels and its many reminiscences of the culture of imperial Rome. Satan opens wide the gates of this secondhand *imperium* to entertain the image of Eve, and her dizzy imagination welcomes the Hell disguised as Heaven in her tempter's rhetoric. She flies away from her rustic garden to thrones and pillared halls where power, the chief delight of frustration, is displayed and adored, and the delay of loving sexual gratification may become, as it is for Hell's monarch, infinite. One of the secrets of Milton's artistic creations is in the way he entitles himself to fulfill his soaring desires by sacrificing, in the works themselves, versions of these desires. It is difficult to believe that the Renaissance Fall of Eve indicated in *Paradise Lost* does not represent a purgation of intimate wishes consummated in the creation of the epic itself—the Lady of Christ's, the Lady of *Comus,* and in the end the Lady Eve of *Paradise Lost.*

After his medieval Fall, however, Adam becomes wonderfully evocative of the seventeenth century. Once intoxicated on the fruit he expresses some new libertine anxieties: he wishes that there were ten forbidden trees in what seems a not altogether jocular concern with making provision for his erotic future; the fires, his joke implies, may never be this intense again. (Not to worry, Adam: Fowler and other

Miltonists—we are not sure who was the first—note that God would eventually fulfill this wish for ten taboo trees by delivering Moses the ten commandments.) The game of sweet reluctant amorous delay now seems to him, as it did to Eve at the beginning of this book, a failure:

> But come, so well refreshed, now let us play,
> As meet is, after such delicious fare;
> For never did thy beauty since the day
> I saw thee first and wedded thee, adorned
> With all perfections, so inflame my sense
> With ardour to enjoy thee, fairer now
> Than ever, bounty of this virtuous tree.
>
> (9.1027–33)

The Renaissance left us thousands of these lyrics of sexual invitation in which the man says to the woman, in so many words, "But come . . . now let us play," but this one is rich with the meaning of a long and lofty poem. It seems at first that Adam might simply be saying that he is as excited now as he was the first time—that it is only that the days of sweet reluctant amorous delay have been impoverished, not that the rites mysterious of connubial love have themselves been improved on. But alas, Eve is "fairer now / Than ever," and we must hear in sorrow that he never before has been so excited. In fallen sexuality, the barrier that preserves and secures desire is no longer delay, the mastered temptation of erotic postponement. The new excitement is moral transgression, the new barrier the law that forbids, taboo itself. God, in other words, now takes his place among those erotic barriers whose presence, when defied, paradoxically serves to protect desire against fatigue. Throughout the poem Milton has striven unto heresy to avoid the usual conflicts between God and sexuality. But that ideal is finally compromised. The last act of intercourse in paradise sets the urgent flesh against the deity, and that, in fact, is its pleasure, "bounty of this virtuous tree." Sexual desire, like the appetite for food, becomes capable of heightened satisfaction with the Fall, and this heightening has a name: "in lust they burn" (9.1015).

Adam seizes her hand, not gently, and leads her to "a shady bank." It is still daylight, as at their first coupling, and they will seize this, too, before it fades. There are no prayers, no delays. They fall upon each other like amorous birds of prey: "There they their fill of love and love's disport / Took largely, of their mutual guilt the seal, /

The solace of their sin" (9.1042–44). The gustatory metaphor reminds us that this sex act is the first in an unended series of repetitions of the Fall. Fallen sex, "their fill" taken largely, is a carnivorous meal; as Adam put it when punning in his invitation lyric, this dalliance "meet is." Milton ends garden eroticism with a sinister transformation of the love hunt.

The course of sexual fruition in his epic may be viewed as a pointed expansion of "To His Coy Mistress." When, before the Fall, there is world enough and time, coyness is no crime, and delay in the game of love is both the government of desire and its major inducement. But as soon as they hear what they are the first to hear, Time's winged chariot, Adam and Eve rather at once their time devour. Time has been hurrying near us human beings for some while now, and modern lovers may no longer hear it as clearly as these do. To this pair the impending catastrophe is not simply or even primarily death, which these sinful lovers have no experience of, just as earlier they "knew not eating death" (9.792), but punishing justice; and their defiance of justice through fugitive intercourse is the "seal" of legitimacy on a confession of "mutual guilt." Their "solace" lies in taking pleasure in sin.

There is much to be said about the restitution of this marriage. Love in *Paradise Lost* is not a minor subject. But we have said enough to conclude that Milton's epic provides a moral and psychological etiology for the manifold postures and dispositions of Renaissance love poetry. It consumes a great tradition, and gives it back to us as representation and as understanding. Wisely Milton captured the beautiful image.

Chronology

1608	Born in London, December 9.
1617	Enters St. Paul's School, London.
1625	Enters Christ's College, Cambridge.
1629	B.A., Cambridge.
1632	M.A., Cambridge.
1632–38	Studies at home in London and at Horton, Buckinghamshire.
1634	Presentation of masque, *Comus*, at Ludlow Castle.
1638–39	Visit to Italy.
1641	*Of Reformation in England.*
1642	*The Reason of Church Government.* Marries Mary Powell, who subsequently returns to her parents.
1643	*The Doctrine and Discipline of Divorce.*
1644	*Areopagitica.*
1645	Mary Powell Milton returns to her husband in London. *Poems of Mr. John Milton, Both English and Latin.*
1649	*The Tenure of Kings and Magistrates.* Becomes Secretary of Foreign Tongues to Cromwell's Council of State.
1651	Latin *Defense of the English People.*
1652	Blindness. Death of Mary Powell Milton and of their son.
1656	Marries Katherine Woodcock.
1658	Death of Katherine Woodcock Milton.
1660	*The Ready and Easy Way to Establish a Free Commonwealth.*
1663	Marries Elizabeth Minshull.
1667	*Paradise Lost* (in ten books).
1671	*Paradise Regained* and *Samson Agonistes.*
1674	*Paradise Lost* (in twelve books). Dies November 8.

Contributors

HAROLD BLOOM, Sterling Professor of the Humanities at Yale University, is the author of *The Anxiety of Influence*, *Poetry and Repression*, and many other volumes of literary criticism. His forthcoming study, *Freud: Transference and Authority*, attempts a full-scale reading of all of Freud's major writings. A MacArthur Prize Fellow, he is general editor of five series of literary criticism published by Chelsea House. During 1987–88, he was appointed Charles Eliot Norton Professor of Poetry at Harvard University.

JOHN HOLLANDER, poet and critic, is A. Bartlett Giamatti Professor of English at Yale University. His books include *Spectral Emanations: New and Selected Poems* and *The Poem of the Mind*.

PATRICIA PARKER is Professor of English and Comparative Literature at the University of Toronto. She is the author of *Inescapable Romance* and the coeditor of *Lyric Poetry: Beyond New Criticism*, *Literary Theory and Renaissance Texts*, and *Shakespeare and the Question of Theory*.

JOHN GUILLORY, Associate Professor of English at Yale University, has written *Poetic Authority* and a forthcoming study of canon-formation.

WILLIAM KERRIGAN, Professor of English at the University of Virginia, has published two critical studies of Milton and a number of essays on Freud and Kierkegaard.

MAUREEN QUILLIGAN is Professor of English at the University of Pennsylvania. She is the author of *The Language of Allegory* and *Milton's Spenser*.

GORDON BRADEN is Associate Professor of English at the University of Virginia. He is the author of *The Classical and English Renaissance Poetry* and *Renaissance Tragedy and the Senecan Tradition*.

Bibliography

Adams, Robert M. *Ikon: John Milton and the Modern Critics.* Ithaca: Cornell University Press, 1955.

Aers, David, and Bob Hodge. " 'Rational Burning': Milton on Sex and Marriage." In *Literature, Language, and Society in England 1580–1680*, edited by David Aers, Bob Hodge, and Gunther Kress. Dublin: Gill & Macmillan, 1981.

Allen, Don Cameron. *The Harmonious Vision: Studies in Milton's Poetry.* Baltimore: The Johns Hopkins University Press, 1953.

Amorose, Thomas. "Milton the Apocalyptic Historian: Competing Genres in *Paradise Lost*, Books 11–12." *Milton Studies* 17 (1983): 141–62.

Anderson, Douglas. "Unfallen Marriage and the Fallen Imagination in *Paradise Lost*." *Studies in English Literature 1500–1900* 26 (1986): 125–44.

Babb, Lawrence. *The Moral Cosmos of* Paradise Lost. East Lansing: Michigan State University Press, 1970.

Barker, Arthur. *Milton and the Puritan Dilemma 1641–1660.* Toronto: University of Toronto Press, 1942.

———. "Structural Pattern in *Paradise Lost*." *Philological Quarterly* 28 (1949): 17–30.

———, ed. *Milton: Modern Essays in Criticism.* New York: Oxford University Press, 1965.

Bennett, Joan S. " 'Go': Milton's Antinomianism and the Separation Scene in *Paradise Lost*, Book 9." *PMLA* 98 (1983): 388–404.

———. "God, Satan, and King Charles: Milton's Royal Portraits." *PMLA* 92 (1977): 441–57.

Berry, Boyd M. *Process of Speech: Puritan Religious Writing and* Paradise Lost. Baltimore: The Johns Hopkins University Press, 1976.

Blessington, Frances C. Paradise Lost *and the Classical Epic.* London: Routledge & Kegan Paul, 1979.

Bloom, Harold. *A Map of Misreading.* New York: Oxford University Press, 1975.

———, ed. *Modern Critical Views: John Milton.* New York: Chelsea House, 1986.

Bradshaw, John. *A Concordance to the Poetical Works of John Milton.* 1894. Reprint. Boston: Longwood, 1977.

Bridges, Robert. *Milton's Prosody.* Oxford: Clarendon Press, 1921.

Brisman, Leslie. *Milton's Poetry of Choice and Its Romantic Heirs.* Ithaca: Cornell University Press, 1973.

Broadbent, J. B. *Some Graver Subjects: An Essay on* Paradise Lost. London: Chatto & Windus, 1960.

Brockbank, Philip. " 'Within the Visible Diurnal Spheare': The Moving World of *Paradise Lost.*" In *Approaches to* Paradise Lost, edited by C. A. Patrides. London: Edward Arnold, 1968.

Brooks, Cleanth. "Eve's Awakening." In *A Shaping Joy.* London: Methuen, 1975.

Bush, Douglas. *Mythology and the Renaissance Tradition in English Poetry.* Minneapolis: University of Minnesota Press, 1932.

———. Paradise Lost *in Our Time: Some Comments.* Ithaca: Cornell University Press, 1945.

Carey, John, and Alastair Fowler. *Poems of Milton.* Longman Annotated English Poets Series. London: Longman, 1980.

Christopher, Georgia B. *Milton and the Science of the Saints.* Princeton: Princeton University Press, 1982.

Cirillo, Albert R. "Noon–Midnight and the Temporal Structure of *Paradise Lost.*" *ELH* 29 (1962): 372–95.

Clark, Donald Lemen. *John Milton at St. Paul's School: A Study of Ancient Rhetoric in English Renaissance Education.* New York: Columbia University Press, 1948.

Colie, Rosalie. "Time and Eternity: Paradox and Structure in *Paradise Lost.*" *Journal of the Warburg and Courtauld Institutes* 23 (1960): 127–38.

Cope, Jackson I. *The Metaphoric Structure of* Paradise Lost. Baltimore: The Johns Hopkins University Press, 1962.

Curry, Walter Clyde. *Milton's Ontology, Cosmology and Physics.* Lexington: University of Kentucky Press, 1957.

Daiches, David. *Milton.* London: Hutchinson, 1957.

Daniells, Roy. *Milton, Mannerism, and Baroque.* Toronto: University of Toronto Press, 1963.

Danielson, Dennis. *Milton's Good God: A Study in Literary Theodicy.* Cambridge: Cambridge University Press, 1982.

Darbishire, Helen. *Milton's* Paradise Lost. Oxford: Clarendon Press, 1951.

Davies, Stevie. *The Idea of Woman in Renaissance Literature: The Feminine Reclaimed.* Brighton: Harvester Press, 1986.

———. *Images of Kingship in* Paradise Lost: *Milton's Politics and Christian Liberty.* Columbia: University of Missouri Press, 1983.

Demaray, John G. *Milton's Theatrical Epic: The Invention and Design of* Paradise Lost. Cambridge: Harvard University Press, 1980.

Diekhoff, John S. *Milton's* Paradise Lost: *A Commentary on the Argument.* New York: Columbia University Press, 1946.

Durling, Robert M. *The Figure of the Poet in the Renaissance Epic.* Cambridge: Harvard University Press, 1965.

Eliot, T. S. "Milton" and "A Note on the Verse of John Milton." In *On Poetry and Poets.* London: Faber & Faber, 1957.

Empson, William. *Milton's God.* London: Chatto & Windus, 1965.

———. *Some Versions of Pastoral.* New York: New Directions, 1950.

Evans, John Martin. Paradise Lost *and the Genesis Tradition.* Oxford: Clarendon Press, 1968.

Evans, Robert C. "*Paradise Lost* and Renaissance Historiography." *Publications of the Mississippi Philological Association* (1984): 69–87.

Ferry, Anne Davidson. *Milton's Epic Voice: The Narrator in* Paradise Lost. Cambridge: Harvard University Press, 1963.

Fish, Stanley. *Surprised by Sin: The Reader in* Paradise Lost. New York: St. Martin's, 1967.

Fletcher, Angus. *Allegory: The Theory of a Symbolic Mode*. Ithaca: Cornell University Press, 1964.

Flinker, Noam. "Father-Daughter Incest in *Paradise Lost.*" *Milton Quarterly* 14 (1980): 116–22.

Fowler, Alastair. *John Milton:* Paradise Lost. Longman Annotated English Poets Series. London: Longman, 1974.

French, J. M. *The Life Records of John Milton*. 4 vols. New Brunswick, N. J.: Rutgers University Press, 1949–66.

Froula, Christine. "When Eve Reads Milton: Undoing the Canonical Economy." In *Canons*, edited by Robert von Hallberg, 149–76. Chicago: University of Chicago Press, 1984.

Frye, Northrop. *The Return of Eden: Five Essays on Milton's Epics*. Toronto: University of Toronto Press, 1965.

Frye, Roland Mushat. *God, Man, and Satan: Patterns of Christian Thought and Life in* Paradise Lost, Pilgrim's Progress *and the Great Theologians*. Princeton: Princeton University Press, 1960.

Fuller, Elizabeth Ely. *Milton's Kinesthetic Vision in* Paradise Lost. Lewisburg, Pa.: Bucknell University Press, 1983.

Gallagher, Philip J. "Milton and Euhemerism: *Paradise Lost* 10.578–84." *Milton Quarterly* 12 (1978): 16–23.

———. " 'Real or Allegoric': The Ontology of Sin and Death in *Paradise Lost.*" *English Literary Renaissance* 6 (1976): 317–33.

Gardner, H. L. *A Reading of* Paradise Lost. Oxford: Clarendon Press, 1965.

Giamatti, A. Bartlett. *The Earthly Paradise and the Renaissance Epic*. Princeton: Princeton University Press, 1966.

Greene, Thomas M. *The Descent from Heaven: A Study in Epic Continuity*. New Haven: Yale University Press, 1963.

Grierson, H. J. C. *Milton and Wordsworth: Poets and Prophets*. Cambridge: Cambridge University Press, 1936.

Griffin, Dustin H. "Milton's Evening." *Milton Studies* 6 (1974): 259–73.

Guillory, John. *Poetic Authority: Spenser, Milton, and Literary History*. New York: Columbia University Press, 1983.

Halkett, John. *Milton and the Idea of Matrimony*. New Haven: Yale University Press, 1970.

Haller, William. "Order and Progress in *Paradise Lost.*" *PMLA* 35 (1920): 218–25.

Harding, Davis P. *The Club of Hercules: Studies in the Classical Background of* Paradise Lost. Urbana: University of Illinois Press, 1962.

———. *Milton and the Renaissance Ovid*. Urbana: University of Illinois Press, 1946.

Hartman, Geoffrey H. "Milton's Counterplot" and "Adam on the Grass with Balsamum." In *Beyond Formalism: Literary Essays 1958–1970*. New Haven: Yale University Press, 1970.

Hill, Christopher. *Milton and the English Revolution*. 1977. Reprint. Harmondsworth: Penguin, 1979.

Hodge, Bob. "Satan and the Revolution of the Saints." In *Literature, Language, and Society in England 1580–1680*, edited by David Aers, Bob Hodge, and Gunther Kress. Dublin: Gill & Macmillan, 1981.

Hollander, John. *The Figure of Echo: A Mode of Allusion in Milton and After.* Berkeley: University of California Press, 1965.

———. *The Untuning of the Sky: Ideas of Music in English Poetry 1500–1700.* Princeton: Princeton University Press, 1961.

Hughes, Merritt Y. "Devils to Adore for Deities." In *Studies in Honor of De Witt T. Starnes,* edited by T. P. Harrison et al., 241–58. Austin: University of Texas Press, 1967.

———. *Ten Perspectives on Milton.* New Haven: Yale University Press, 1965.

Hunter, G. K. *Paradise Lost.* Unwin Critical Library Series. London: Allen & Unwin, 1980.

Hunter, William B. "Milton and Thrice-Great Hermes." *Journal of English and Germanic Philology* 45 (1946): 327–36.

———. "Milton's Materialistic Life Principle." *Journal of English and Germanic Philology* 45 (1946): 68–76.

Hunter, William B., C. A. Patrides, and J. H. Adamson, eds. *Bright Essence: Studies in Milton's Theology.* Salt Lake City: University of Utah Press, 1971.

Hunter, William B., Jr., et al., eds. *A Milton Encyclopedia.* Lewisburg, Pa.: Bucknell University Press, 1978–83.

Ide, Richard S. "On the Uses of Elizabethan Drama: The Revaluation of Epic in *Paradise Lost.*" *Milton Studies* 17 (1983): 121–40.

Kermode, Frank. "Milton's Hero." *Review of English Studies* 4 (1953): 317–30.

———, ed. *The Living Milton.* London: Routledge & Kegan Paul, 1960.

Kerrigan, William. *The Prophetic Milton.* Charlottesville: University Press of Virginia, 1974.

———. *The Sacred Complex: On the Psychogenesis of* Paradise Lost. Cambridge: Harvard University Press, 1983.

Knight, Douglas. "The Dramatic Center of *Paradise Lost.*" *Stuttgarter Arbeiten zur Germanistic* 63 (1964): 44–59.

Knight, G. Wilson. *The Burning Oracle: Studies in the Poetry of Action.* London: Oxford University Press, 1939.

———. *Chariot of Wrath: The Message of John Milton to Democracy at War.* London: Faber & Faber, 1942.

Knott, John Ray. *Milton's Pastoral Vision.* Chicago: University of Chicago Press, 1971.

Kranidas, Thomas. *The Fierce Equation: A Study of Milton's Decorum.* The Hague: Mouton, 1965.

———, ed. *New Essays on* Paradise Lost. Berkeley: University of California Press, 1971.

Lawry, Jon S. *The Shadow of Heaven: Matter and Stance in Milton's Poetry.* Ithaca: Cornell University Press, 1968.

Leavis, F. R. "Milton's Verse." In *Revaluation.* London: Chatto & Windus, 1956.

Le Comte, Edward. *Milton and Sex.* New York: Columbia University Press, 1978.

Lewalski, Barbara Kieffer. "The Genres of *Paradise Lost*: Literary Genre as a Means of Accommodation." *Milton Studies* 17 (1983): 75–103.

―――. "Structure and the Symbolism of Vision in Michael's Prophecy, *Paradise Lost*, 11–12." *Philological Quarterly* 42 (1963): 23–35.

Lewis, C. S. *A Preface to* Paradise Lost. London: Oxford University Press, 1942.

Lieb, Michael. *The Dialectics of Creation: Patterns of Birth and Regeneration in* Paradise Lost. Amherst: University of Massachusetts Press, 1970.

―――. *Poetics of the Holy: A Reading of* Paradise Lost. Chapel Hill: University of North Carolina Press, 1981.

Lovejoy, Arthur O. "Milton and the Paradox of the Fortunate Fall." *ELH* 4 (1937): 16–179.

MacCabe, Colin. " 'So truth be in the field': Milton's Use of Language." In *Teaching the Text,* edited by Susanne Kappeler and Norman Bryson, 18–34. London: Routledge & Kegan Paul, 1983.

MacCaffrey, Isabel Gamble. Paradise Lost *as "Myth."* Cambridge: Harvard University Press, 1959.

MacCallum, H. R. "Milton and Figurative Interpretation of the Bible." *University of Toronto Quarterly* 31 (1962): 397–415.

―――. "Milton and Sacred History: Books 11 and 12 of *Paradise Lost.*" In *Essays in English Literature from the Renaissance to the Victorian Age Presented to A. S. P. Woodhouse,* edited by Millar MacLure and F. W. Watt. Toronto: University of Toronto Press, 1964.

McColley, Diane Kelsey. *Milton's Eve.* Urbana: University of Illinois Press, 1983.

Madsen, William G. "The Fortunate Fall in *Paradise Lost.*" *MLN* 74 (1959): 103–5.

―――. *From Shadowy Types to Truth: Studies in Milton's Symbolism.* New Haven: Yale University Press, 1968.

Major, John M., ed. *Milton Essays and Reviews.* Special Issue. *English Language Notes* 19, no. 3 (March 1982).

Manuel, M. *The Seventeenth-Century Critics and Biographers of Milton.* Trivandrum, India: University of Kerala Press, 1962.

Marshall, W. H. "*Paradise Lost: Felix Culpa* and the Problem of Structure." *MLN* 76 (1961): 15–20.

Martz, Louis L. *The Paradise Within: Studies in Vaughan, Traherne, and Milton.* New Haven: Yale University Press, 1964.

―――. *Poet of Exile: A Study of Milton's Poetry.* New Haven: Yale University Press, 1980.

―――, ed. *Milton: A Collection of Critical Essays.* Englewood Cliffs, N.J.: Prentice-Hall, 1966.

Milner, Andrew. *John Milton and the English Revolution.* London: Macmillan, 1981.

Miner, Earl. "The Reign of Narrative in *Paradise Lost.*" *Milton Studies* 17 (1983): 3–25.

―――. *The Restoration Mode from Milton to Dryden.* Princeton: Princeton University Press, 1974.

Murrin, Michael. "The Language of Milton's Heaven." *Modern Philology* 74 (1977): 350–65.

Neuse, Richard. "Milton and Spenser: The Virgilian Triad Revisited." *ELH* 45 (1978): 606–39.

Nicholson, Marjorie Hope. "Milton and Hobbes." *Studies in Philology* 23 (1926): 405–33.

――――. "The Spirit World of Milton and More." *Studies in Philology* 22 (1925): 433–52.

――――. "The Telescope and Imagination." *Modern Philology* 32 (1935): 233–60.

Norbrook, David. "The Politics of Milton's Early Poetry." In *Poetry and Politics in the English Renaissance*. London: Routledge & Kegan Paul, 1984.

Norford, Don Parry. "The Sacred Head: Milton's Solar Mysticism." *Milton Studies* 9 (1976): 37–75.

Nuttall, A. D. *Overheard by God: Fiction and Prayer in Herbert, Milton, Dante, and St. John*. London: Methuen, 1980.

Osgood, Charles Grosvenor. *The Classical Mythology of Milton's English Poems*. 1899. Reprint. New York: Haskell House, 1964.

Parker, Patricia. *Inescapable Romance: Studies in the Poetics of a Mode*. Princeton: Princeton University Press, 1979.

Patrides, C. A. *Milton and the Christian Tradition*. Oxford: Clarendon Press, 1966.

――――. " 'Something Like Prophetic Strain': Apocalyptic Configurations in Milton." *English Language Notes* 19, no. 3 (1982): 3–25.

――――, ed. *Milton's Epic Poetry: Essays on* Paradise Lost *and* Paradise Regained. Harmondsworth: Penguin, 1967.

Peter, John D. *A Critique of* Paradise Lost. New York: Columbia University Press, 1960.

Quilligan, Maureen. *Milton's Spenser: The Politics of Reading*. Ithaca: Cornell University Press, 1983.

Revard, Stella P. "Milton's Muse and the Daughters of Memory." *English Literary Renaissance* 9 (1979): 432–41.

――――. *The War in Heaven:* Paradise Lost *and the Tradition of Satan's Rebellion*. Ithaca: Cornell University Press, 1980.

Rajan, Balachandra. "Milton, Humanism, and the Concept of Piety." In *Poetic Traditions of the English Renaissance,* edited by Maynard Mack and George DeForest Lord, 251–69. New Haven: Yale University Press, 1982.

――――. Paradise Lost *and the Seventeenth-Century Reader*. London: Chatto & Windus, 1947.

Richmond, Hugh M. *The Christian Revolutionary: John Milton*. Berkeley: University of California Press, 1972.

Ricks, Christopher. *Milton's Grand Style*. Oxford: Clarendon Press, 1963.

――――. "Sound and Sense in *Paradise Lost*." *Essays by Divers Hands* 39 (1977): 92–111.

Riggs, William G. *The Christian Poet in* Paradise Lost. Berkeley: University of California Press, 1972.

――――. "The Poet and Satan in *Paradise Lost*." In *Milton Studies II*, edited by James D. Simmonds. Pittsburgh, Pa.: University of Pittsburgh Press, 1970.

Robson, W. W. "*Paradise Lost*: Changing Interpretations and Controversy." In *The New Pelican Guide to English Literature, III: From Donne to Marvell*, edited by Boris Ford, 239–59. Harmondsworth: Penguin, 1982.

Rosenblatt, Jason P. " 'Audacious Neighborhood': Idolatry in *Paradise Lost*, Book 1." *Philological Quarterly* 54 (1975): 553–68.

Ross, Alexander. *Mystagogus Poeticus or the Muses Interpreter*. London, 1648. Reprint. New York: Garland, 1976.

Ross, Malcolm M. "Milton and the Protestant Aesthetic." In *Poetry and Dogma.* New Brunswick, N.J.: Rutgers University Press, 1954.

———. *Milton's Royalism.* Ithaca: Cornell University Press, 1943.

Ryken, Leland. *The Apocalyptic Vision in* Paradise Lost. Ithaca: Cornell University Press, 1970.

Samuel, Irene. *Dante and Milton: The* Commedia *and* Paradise Lost. Ithaca: Cornell University Press, 1966.

———. *Plato and Milton.* Ithaca: Cornell University Press, 1947.

Sewell, Arthur. *A Study in Milton's Christian Doctrine.* London: Oxford University Press, 1939.

Shawcross, John T. "The Balanced Structure of *Paradise Lost.*" *Studies in Philology* 62 (1965): 696–718.

———. "The Chronology of Milton's Major Poems." *PMLA* 76 (1961): 45–58.

———. "The Metaphor of Inspiration in *Paradise Lost.*" In *Th' Upright Heart and Pure,* edited by Amadeus P. Fiore. Pittsburgh, Pa.: Duquesne University Press, 1967.

———. *Milton: A Bibliography for the Years 1624–1700.* Binghamton, N.Y.: Center for Medieval and Early Renaissance Studies, 1984.

———. *With Mortal Voice: The Creation of* Paradise Lost. Lexington: University Press of Kentucky, 1982.

Shoaf, R. A. *Milton, Poet of Duality: A Study of Semiosis in the Poetry and Prose.* New Haven: Yale University Press, 1985.

Sloane, Thomas O. *Donne, Milton, and the End of Humanist Rhetoric.* Berkeley: University of California Press, 1985.

Sprott, Ernest S. *Milton's Art of Prosody.* Oxford: Clarendon Press, 1958.

Steadman, John M. *Milton and the Renaissance Hero.* Oxford: Clarendon Press, 1967.

———. *Milton's Biblical and Classical Imagery.* Pittsburgh, Pa.: Duquesne University Press, 1984.

———. *Milton's Epic Characters: Image and Idol.* Chapel Hill: University of North Carolina Press, 1959.

Stein, Arnold. *Answerable Style: Essays on* Paradise Lost. Minneapolis: University of Minnesota Press, 1953.

———. *The Art of Presence: The Poet and* Paradise Lost. Berkeley: University of California Press, 1977.

Summers, Joseph H. *The Muse's Method: An Introduction to* Paradise Lost. Cambridge: Harvard University Press, 1962.

Svendson, Kester. *Milton and Science.* Cambridge: Harvard University Press, 1956.

Swaim, Kathleen M. "The Mimesis of Accommodation in Book 3 of *Paradise Lost.*" *Philological Quarterly* 63 (1984): 461–75.

Tillyard, E. M. W. *The English Epic and Its Background.* London: Chatto & Windus, 1954.

———. *The Miltonic Setting, Past and Present.* London: Chatto & Windus, 1957.

———. *Studies in Milton.* London: Chatto & Windus, 1951.

Tolliver, Harold E. "Complicity of Voice in *Paradise Lost.*" *Modern Language Quarterly* 25 (1964): 153–70.

Tuve, Rosemond. "Baroque and Mannerist Milton." *Journal of English and Germanic Philology* 60 (1961): 817–33.

————. *Images and Themes in Five Poems by Milton*. Cambridge: Harvard University Press, 1957.

Waldock, A. J. Paradise Lost *and Its Critics*. Cambridge: Cambridge University Press, 1947.

Watkins, Walter B. *An Anatomy of Milton's Verse*. 1955. Reprint. Hamden, Conn.: Shoe String, 1965.

Weiskel, Thomas. *The Romantic Sublime: Studies in the Structure and Psychology of Transcendence*. Baltimore: Johns Hopkins University Press, 1976.

Whaler, James. "The Miltonic Simile." *PMLA* 46 (1931): 1034–74.

Williamson, George. *Milton and Others*. Rev. ed. Chicago: University of Chicago Press, 1970.

————. *Seventeenth-Century Contexts*. Rev. ed. London: University of Chicago Press, 1969.

Wilson, A. N. *The Life of John Milton*. Oxford: Oxford University Press, 1983.

Wittreich, Joseph Anthony, Jr. " 'All Angelic Natures Joined in One': Epic Convention and Prophetic Interiority in the Council Scenes of *Paradise Lost*." *Milton Studies* 17 (1983): 43–74.

————. *Visionary Poetics: Milton's Tradition and His Legacy*. San Marino, Cal.: Huntington Library Press, 1979.

————, ed. *Calm of Mind*. Cleveland, Ohio: Case Western Reserve University Press, 1971.

————, ed. *Milton and the Line of Vision*. Madison: University of Wisconsin Press, 1975.

————, ed. *The Romantics on Milton*. Cleveland, Ohio: Case Western Reserve University Press, 1975.

Woodhouse, A. S. P. "Notes on Milton's View of Creation: The Initial Phases." *Philological Quarterly* 28 (1949): 211–36.

————. "Pattern in *Paradise Lost*." *University of Toronto Quarterly* 22 (1952–53): 109–27.

Wooten, John. "The Comic Milton and Italian Burlesque Poet." *Cithara* 22, no. 1 (November 1982): 3–12.

————. "From Purgatory to the Paradise of Fools: Dante, Ariosto, and Milton." *ELH* 49, no. 4 (1982): 741–50.

Wright, B. A. *Milton's* Paradise Lost. London: Methuen, 1962.

Acknowledgments

"Milton and Transumption" (originally entitled "Milton and His Precursors") by Harold Bloom from *A Map of Misreading* by Harold Bloom, © 1975 by Oxford University Press, Inc. Reprinted by permission.

"Echo Schematic" by John Hollander from *The Figure of Echo: A Mode of Allusion in Milton and After* by John Hollander, © 1981 by the Regents of the University of California. Reprinted by permission of the University of California Press.

"Eve, Evening, and the Labor of Reading in *Paradise Lost*" by Patricia Parker from *English Literary Renaissance* 9, no. 2 (Spring 1979), © 1979 by *English Literary Renaissance* 9, no. 2 (Spring 1979), © 1979 by *English Literary Renaissance*. Reprinted by permission.

"Ithuriel's Spear: History and the Language of Accommodation" by John Guillory from *Poetic Authority: Spenser, Milton, and Literary History* by John Guillory, © 1983 by Columbia University Press. Reprinted by permission.

" 'One First Matter All': Spirit as Energy" by William Kerrigan from *The Sacred Complex: On the Psychogenesis of* Paradise Lost by William Kerrigan, © 1983 by the President and Fellows of Harvard College. Reprinted by permission of Harvard University Press.

"The Gender of Milton's Muse and the Problem of the Fit Reader" (originally entitled "The Gender of the Reader") by Maureen Quilligan from *Milton's Spenser: The Politics of Reading* by Maureen Quilligan, © 1983 by Cornell University Press. Reprinted by permission of the publisher.

"Milton's Coy Eve: *Paradise Lost* and Renaissance Love Poetry" by William Kerrigan and Gordon Braden from *ELH* 53, no. 1 (Spring 1986), © 1986 by the Johns Hopkins University Press, Baltimore/London. Reprinted by permission.

Index

171